New Directions for
Higher Education

Martin Kramer and
Judith Block McLaughlin
CO-EDITORS-IN-CHIEF

International Collaborations: Opportunities, Strategies, Challenges

Pamela L. Eddy

EDITOR

DISCARD

Number 150 • Summer 2010
Jossey-Bass
San Francisco

INTERNATIONAL COLLABORATIONS: OPPORTUNITIES, STRATEGIES, CHALLENGES
Pamela L. Eddy (ed.)
New Directions for Higher Education, no. 150
Martin Kramer, Judith Block McLaughlin, Co-Editors-in-Chief

Microfilm copies of issues and articles are available in 16mm and 35mm, as well as microfiche in 105mm, through University Microfilms Inc., 300 North Zeeb Road, Ann Arbor, MI 48106-1346.

NEW DIRECTIONS FOR HIGHER EDUCATION (ISSN 0271-0560, electronic ISSN 1536-0741) is part of The Jossey-Bass Higher and Adult Education Series and is published quarterly by Wiley Subscription Services, Inc., A Wiley Company, at Jossey-Bass, 989 Market Street, San Francisco, CA 94103-1741. Periodicals Postage Paid at San Francisco, California, and at additional mailing offices. POSTMASTER: Send address changes to New Directions for Higher Education, Jossey-Bass, 989 Market Street, San Francisco, CA 94103-1741.

New Directions for Higher Education is indexed in Current Index to Journals in Education (ERIC); Higher Education Abstracts.

SUBSCRIPTIONS cost $89 for individuals and $244 for institutions, agencies, and libraries. See ordering information page at end of journal.

EDITORIAL CORRESPONDENCE should be sent to the Co-Editors-in-Chief, Martin Kramer, 2807 Shasta Road, Berkeley, CA 94708-2011 and Judith Block McLaughlin, Harvard GSE, Gutman 435, Cambridge, MA 02138.

Cover photograph © Digital Vision

www.josseybass.com

CONTENTS

PART ONE

Setting the Context

EDITOR'S NOTES

The world is getting smaller. The ability to communicate with colleagues around the globe makes collaborations easier and the exchange of ideas and knowledge faster. Travel between countries is more accessible today than in the past. To date, writing on international education has focused most on the acculturation and assimilation of international students into U.S. colleges and universities (Al-Sharideh and Goe, 1998). The concept of internationalization, however, has begun to move beyond these historical concepts of partnerships and exchanges.

Because individuals and institutions bring different interpretations and assumptions to these joint efforts, Knight (2009) argues that conversations about internationalization require agreement on the definition of terms. Recent definitions break into two camps: "internationalization at home" and "cross-border education" (Knight, p. 115). The former term refers to initiatives that are campus-based and highlight international dimensions in classroom teaching, cultural events, and with local ethnic groups, including international students on campus. The latter term references activities that are off-campus, such as study abroad, joint degrees between and among countries, or faculty mobility. Current external pressures on U.S. colleges and universities now encourage U.S. institutions to investigate and pursue international partnerships as a way to increase revenues and to support curriculum for student skill development of global competencies (McMurtrie and Wheeler, 2008), predominately placing them in the context of cross-border projects.

International collaborations occur within an organizational context that impacts administrative practices as well as faculty work. Partnerships among institutions require looking at the motivation of each of the institutions involved. Often, the partners have not overtly addressed issues of unequal resources or power bases (Amey, Eddy, Campbell, and Watson, 2008) or paid sufficient attention to assumptions regarding faculty engagement in the delivery of the programs (O'Hara, 2009). Typically, faculty involved in collaborations need to mediate their work through organizational structures in place (Slater, 2006) and this results in unpredictable outcomes based on institutional contexts. Recent research reports a continued lack of involvement of U.S. faculty in international research or teaching (e.g., collaboration with international scholars, research that is international in scope, publishing in foreign countries, or teaching courses with an emphasis on international content) (Finkelstein, Walker, and Chen, 2009; O'Hara). This volume intends to

New Directions for Higher Education, no. 150, Summer 2010 © Wiley Periodicals, Inc.
Published online in Wiley InterScience (www.interscience.wiley.com) • DOI: 10.1002/he.385

provide a framework for discussion about international collaborations to illuminate the challenges and supports found in best practices.

When innovation is important and resources are scarce, partnerships provide options beyond what schools and colleges can accomplish individually, thereby greatly benefiting institutional members. Partnerships can enable greater educational access and opportunity for students, resulting in a greater public good as well (Chin, Bell, Munby, and Hutchinson, 2004). International collaborations have an added layer of complexity because they are mediated through the use of different languages and cultures (Scarino, Crichton, and Woods, 2007). Colleges involved in international efforts range from research universities with long traditions of study abroad programming and research collaborations to community colleges seeking to educate global citizens (Boggs and Irwin, 2007). It is critical for both leaders and faculty to have an understanding of the issues and strategies involved in these types of linkages.

This volume of *New Directions for Higher Education* explores what it means to collaborate in international contexts. Part One of the volume provides context for the issues facing institutions as they look to international partners and to global markets. This Editor's Notes establishes the framework regarding international education overall and identifies key themes in the research. Chapter One by Tubbeh and Williams provides more details on current dialogues regarding international education, particularly the roles and influences partners bring to international collaborations and the challenges facing them.

Part Two of the volume contains a number of case examples of collaborations in practice. Chapter Two presents examples of institutional collaborations in Ireland and situates these partnerships in the larger European Union context. In Chapter Three, Holland reviews the program offerings that a small community college in Canada delivers in China, providing a historical backdrop for the current partnership. China serves as the international partner highlighted in Chapter Four. Here, Jie uses game theory to describe the collaborative efforts of two premier colleges as they enter into a joint degree program.

The last section, Part Three, considers stakeholders in the process of international collaboration, namely administrators, faculty, and students. Each of these constituencies brings differing needs to the venture and different assumptions of how to operationalize the collaborative. In Chapter Five, Amey uses four international collaborations to showcase the changes in administrative practices and processes that resulted from these joint efforts. Faculty work with international partners impacted departmental operations with respect to resources, absence from the home campus, and alignment with departmental and college strategic goals. Chapter Six focuses on faculty initiatives at the individual, course, and program level due to participation in cross-border collaborations. Cooper and Mitsunaga investigate faculty motivations for initial participation and present strategies for others seeking to engage in partnerships. In Chapter Seven, Brewer reflects on internationalization efforts at a liberal arts college. Expansion of faculty development efforts serve to institutionalize global efforts, allowing home-based students exposure to global experiences through internationalization of the curriculum. A case study serves to highlight an example of these efforts. The focus in Chapter Eight is on the student experience in international education programs. Kelly discusses how the increased use of technology allows students to stay connected with their home institution, family, and friends and ultimately how these connections alter the experience. College faculty can thus develop different means of capitalizing on these connections. Finally, in Chapter Nine, Holly offers an outline to strategize for the future as institutions look to form collaborations internationally. Each chapter includes campus-based examples, offers best practices, or covers implications for practice and policy in international collaborations.

Throughout this volume, several key themes inform the research and writing. They include:

- An examination of motivating factors for collaboration, paying attention to institutional and faculty rewards
- A theoretical framework to analyze varying forms of collaborations
- An examination of the underlying assumptions regarding collaborations and impacts on faculty teaching and collaborative research
- An emphasis on the power dynamics in operation within collaborative efforts for both institutions and faculty
- A questioning of the issues to address prior to entering into a collaborative effort and strategies to overcome known barriers

This book, thus, has both a scholarly and a practical bent. For scholars, the volume advances the knowledge about the issues involved with international collaborations and, indeed, with institutional partnerships of all kinds. But the main target audience for this volume is practitioners, both those who lead international collaborative efforts and those who teach in them. By examining the experiences of many different institutions with international partnerships, this book offers important lessons about the challenges and opportunities in this work. The insights, experiences, and research findings presented here can help universities with a goal of increasing their reach into global markets to anticipate problems, ask the right questions in formatting partnerships, and educate those within their campus communities regarding the pressing need to become more globally aware.

References

Al-Sharideh, K. A., and Goe, W. R. "Ethnic Communities Within the University: As Examination of Factors Influencing the Personal Adjustment of International Students." *Research in Higher Education*, 1998, 39(6), 699–725.

Amey, M. J., Eddy, P. L., Campbell, T., and Watson, J. *The Role of Social Capital in Facilitating Partnerships.* Paper presented at the 2008 Council for the Study of Community College Annual Conference, Philadelphia, Pa., April 2008.

Boggs, G. R., and Irwin, J. "What Every Community College Needs to Know: Building Leadership for International Education." *New Directions for Community Colleges,* no. 138. San Francisco: Jossey-Bass, 2007.

Chin, P., Bell, K. S., Munby, H., and Hutchinson, N. L. "Epistemological Appropriation in One High School Student's Learning in Cooperative Education." *American Educational Research Journal,* 2004, *41*(2), 401–417.

Finkelstein, M. J., Walker, E., and Chen, R. *The Internationalization of the American Faculty: Where Are We? What Drives or Deters Us?* Unpublished report, Seton Hall University, South Orange, N.J., 2009.

Knight, J. "New Developments and Unintended Consequences: Whither Thou Goest, Internationalization?" In R. Bhandari and S. Laughlin (eds.), *Higher Education on the Move: New Developments in Global Mobility.* New York: The Institute of International Education, 2009.

McMurtrie, B., and Wheeler, D. "Leaders Urge Colleges to Think Globally Despite Economic Crisis." *Chronicle of Higher Education,* 2008, *55*(13), A25.

O'Hara, S. "Internationalizing the Academy: The Impact of Scholar Mobility." In R. Bhandari and S. Laughlin (eds.), *Higher Education on the Move: New Developments in Global Mobility.* New York: The Institute of International Education, 2009.

Scarino, A., Crichton, J., and Woods, M. "The Role of Language and Culture in Open Learning in International Collaborative Programmes." *Open Learning,* 2007, *22*(3), 219–233.

Slater, J. J. "Creating Collaborations: From Isolationism to Community." *International Journal of Educational Management,* 2006, *20*(3), 215–223.

PAMELA L. EDDY *is associate professor of Educational Policy, Planning, and Leadership at the College of William and Mary. She was a 2009 Fulbright Scholar at Dublin Institute of Technology, Dublin, Ireland. She has published articles on partnerships and collaborations that focus on institutional projects and on faculty working groups.*

NEW DIRECTIONS FOR HIGHER EDUCATION • DOI: 10.1002/he

1

A key step in the partnership process with cross-border coalitions involves addressing contradictory dynamics and creating a shared sense of understanding.

Framing Issues of International Education

Leila Tubbeh, Jobila Williams

"It can be said, and has been said by many, that the internationalization of education is inevitable, as the advancement of knowledge and understanding is a global enterprise that has no borders" (de Wit, 2002, p. 95). The exponential expansion of new technologies, the inception of an increasingly mobile society, and the marketization of knowledge in Thomas Friedman's (2007) *flat*, globalized world have fanned the already fiery demand for global higher education. According to Stewart and Kagan (2005), the global demand for higher education will increase from ninety-seven million in 2000 to 263 million by 2025, and seven million of those students will gain an education through online means, with students often taking these online courses from providers in other countries. Currently, more than one million students study at an institution outside their national borders, representing a tenfold increase over the last thirty years alone (Altbach, 1998; Husén, 1996). In an era of globalization that "brings multiple diverse economies, political systems, countries, and cultures across the world into one single free market economic structure," institutions of higher education must seek opportunities to diversify and internationalize the student experience both within the curriculum and through global experiences as a means of maintaining or gaining a competitive edge in the global market (Tedrow and Mabokela, 2007, p. 164). Another push for international expansion of education occurs during financially stringent times. As government funding becomes less reliable, institutions of higher education must seek innovative avenues to generate revenue, often looking beyond borders to do so (Hodson and Thomas, 2001; Labi, 2009; Schugurensky, 2003; Zahn, Sandell, and Lindsay, 2007).

New Directions for Higher Education, no. 150, Summer 2010 © Wiley Periodicals, Inc.
Published online in Wiley InterScience (www.interscience.wiley.com) • DOI: 10.1002/he.386

Various motivations drive international ventures, such as expanding access to higher education, generating profits, increasing visibility and competitiveness in the international higher education arena, and preparing and providing the next generation with skills and knowledge to navigate a global community and workforce (Chapman and Austin, 2002; Heffernan and Poole, 2005). Institutions may be driven by political, economic, sociocultural, and academic rationales to partner across borders (de Wit, 2002). Efforts to internationalize higher education can include international activity through national and institutional entities, partnerships, and joint initiatives; student, scholar, and staff mobility and exchange; open communication systems and outputs like Web sites, research information, and the media; knowledge-sharing through research and partnerships; and international programming and curriculum (Turner and Robson, 2008, pp. 12–14). Tedrow and Mabokela (2007) define these different forms of partnerships as "formally developed relations between institutions where the participating partners derive mutual benefit from the involvement" (p. 160). According to Magrath (as cited in de Wit, 2002), these international partnerships will shift in the coming years from *cottage industries* to *multinational consortia* as a consequence of globalization.

Key to understanding international educational partnerships is knowledge of how these partnerships are established. Who is involved? Who are the stakeholders? Who should be at the table for discussion and implementation? What are the various forms of *partnerships*? What are some of the challenges and successes? What are the consequences, implications, and outcomes? Lastly, how do we ensure sustainability, and why is sustainability important? Thinking about the answers to these questions in the planning phase can lead to effective and successful collaborative experiences.

Stakeholders and Constituents in International Education Partnerships

International education involves partnerships established by a myriad of stakeholders, including government-funded agencies and foundations, nonprofit organizations, private sector entities, institutions, and universities. According to Altbach (1998), governmental policies and academic institutions "play a crucial role in determining the nature of foreign study opportunities and in shaping the realities of the experience" (p. 151). Thus, partnerships may begin with macro-level stakeholders at the governmental or institutional level forming policies that then funnel down to implementers like faculty and departmental programs. For instance, European institutions of higher education have taken a macro-level view of partnerships with the onset of the Bologna Process. Through coordinated efforts several well-established organizations have joined forces to support the cooperative process, including the European Association for International Education, the German Academic Exchange Service (DAAD), the Netherlands Organization for International Cooperation in Higher Education, and CampusFrance (Labi, 2009).

NEW DIRECTIONS FOR HIGHER EDUCATION • DOI: 10.1002/he

In other cases, initiatives spring from the ground up and must be approved by top administration. In either situation, it is important to ensure that all stakeholders agree to the terms of the partnership; have an understanding of the expectations, goals, benefits, and partnership roles; and have built a partnership on trust, commitment, and communication (Heffernan and Poole, 2005). Without a strong foundation and clearly defined roles for each participant, the collaboration will not be sustainable and in some cases may never move beyond the concept phase to fruition. Moreover, not only do governmental entities and institutional leaders have a stake in international partnerships, but faculty, students, and administrators are key constituents affected by and interested in international educational partnerships (Taylor, 2003). Each of these stakeholder groups experience internationalization efforts uniquely.

Faculty. In an age of globalization, it is inevitable that faculty members will be forced to globalize their disciplinary perspectives: "some faculty will even become citizens of time rather than place [such that] invisible colleges in those disciplines now mostly confined to national boundaries will likely expand, resulting in the measurement of prestige and status by one's colleagues worldwide" (Tierney, 1999, as cited in Morey, 2003, p. 82). Mason (1998) agrees, adding that "the areas of curriculum most appropriate for a global content (where perspectives from a global student body, or material reflecting global considerations, is relevant), will be the first showcase successes" in globalizing disciplines in higher education for international partnerships (p. 55).

Furthermore, faculty members are increasingly being scouted from abroad so that faculty values align with and sustain an institution's international goals (Turner and Robson, 2008). In the case of Pittsburgh State, more than forty of the institution's three-hundred faculty members were born in other countries, allowing the university to leverage its faculty members' personal and professional ties abroad to build strong international partnerships (NAFSA, 2008). Given the changing nature of academe as a globalized entity, international education partners must look to the faculty as a distinct stakeholder, constituent, ally, and contributor to international efforts—and when faculty members do contribute to international education partnerships, these efforts must be rewarded, as in the case of Nebraska Wesleyan University, which provides faculty members 100 percent of their salary instead of two-thirds if they spend their sabbatical year outside the United States (NAFSA, 2008).

Administrators. The administrative leaders and international office personnel of an institution are frequently charged with the burdensome task of developing, implementing, and maintaining international education partnerships in various forms. These practitioners must have the intercultural sensitivity and interpersonal competence to effectively negotiate and maintain healthy partnerships, the etiquette to decline or terminate unhealthy partnerships, and the foresight to take precautions against potential problems and mitigating circumstances. Effective administrators of international partnerships must be part diplomat, part attorney, part counselor, part soothsayer. Thus, it is essential that administrators serve an integral role in the early creation and negotiation phases of international partnerships, as these practitioners have the natural skill-set and requisite experience to carry out the development of the partnership successfully within a given timeframe.

Students. In international education partnerships "designed to prepare students for careers in the global economy and to facilitate greater intercultural understanding, tolerance and respect," students unquestionably play a crucial role in the health, sustainability, and learning outcomes of the partnership (Turner and Robson, 2008, p. 58). Students are frequently the benefactors of international education partnerships at the institutional level. Furthermore, international students from the United States and abroad serve as cultural ambassadors in a reciprocal environs of educational exchange (Eggins, 2003). These students represent a new generation of highly mobile, globally competent individuals prepared to meet the economic, technological, and cultural challenges of a flat world.

Types of International Education Partnerships

International education partnerships, also referred to as cross-border or transnational collaborations, exist in various forms. These include, but are not limited to, faculty and student exchange programs, study abroad opportunities, joint research ventures, international degree offerings, and distance education (Eggins, 2003; Labi, 2009). De Wit (2002) states that these "strategic partnerships in research, teaching, and transfer of knowledge, between universities and of universities with business and beyond national borders, will be the future for higher education in order to manage the challenges that globalization will place on it" (p. 205).

Study Abroad and Exchange. Study abroad and faculty/student exchange programs are two of the most popular forms of international education partnerships. The U.S. Department of State's Fulbright Program administered through the Institute of International Education is the largest U.S. international exchange program. Fulbright awarded approximately six thousand grants to students, teachers, professionals, and scholars in 2008, investing more than $275.4 million in this programming ("About Fulbright," 2009). Governments abroad also invest in student exchange and study abroad. For example, in 2008, the Spanish Ministry of Education, Science and Innovation, and Foreign Affairs invested approximately $3 million in the establishment of a foundation to help promote higher education abroad (Labi, 2009). This organization is just one of many established to help increase global exposure for higher education institutions.

In addition to government programs, institutions of higher education as well as for-profit and not-for-profit organizations maintain their own study abroad and exchange programs, making study abroad a big business and a source of revenue generation at a time of economic upheaval in higher education. For-profit and not-for-profit organizations called third-party providers, like the American Institute for Foreign Study (AIFS) and the Council on International Educational Exchange (CIEE), work with institutions abroad to bundle study abroad experiences for American students.

Joint Research Ventures. Institutions or individual faculty members may also choose to collaborate with partners from abroad on joint research ventures. Bringing an international perspective to research enhances its applicability in an increasingly globalized world and strengthens the framework of the research through diverse lenses. Shaw (2006) likens developing a joint research venture to the life-cycle stages of birth, childhood, adulthood, and death: one must "identify potential research colleagues, communicate with regard for cultural differences, identify a global problem to investigate, establish a working relationship, design a mutually beneficial project, set goals and divide the labor, present and disseminate the results, and terminate or maintain partnerships" (p. 441). Joint research ventures are effective at internationalizing an institution, its curriculum, and its contributing scholarship, and such ventures are personally and professionally meaningful for individual faculty members.

International Degree Offerings. An exciting form of international education partnerships is the international degree. Universities may partner with institutions abroad to develop a shared degree program or may offer its own degree program located at an international university. In 2006, the University of New Hampshire offered its first international degree in Management of Technology in Seoul, South Korea ("UNH Begins First International Degree Program," 2006). The Whittemore School of Business and Economics manages the program, and Whittemore faculty members as well as faculty members from six of Seoul's top business schools provide content instruction and work collaboratively on research. The College of William & Mary and St. Andrews University are currently developing a joint-degree program to be launched in the 2010–2011 academic year, whereby students will study at both institutions and receive a single degree bearing seals of the two universities (Crump, 2008).

Distance Education. International education partnerships are, in part, an outcome of enhanced technologies that have changed the face of higher education by moving coursework online, computerizing presentations, providing online communication through e-mail and discussion boards, and digitizing libraries and databases (Mason, 1998). The introduction of such technologies have made possible distance education programs and *open universities* that emphasize independent study of specially prepared learning materials in an online environment, ultimately bringing together students and teachers from around the world (Kaye and Rumble, 1996).

Partnership Agreements. Although many forms of international partnerships exist, de Wit (2002) explains that there is a standard procedure for formalizing an international partnership contract:

Traditionally, institutions of higher education establish their international linkages with a partner institution abroad via bilateral agreements, memoranda of understanding, and letters of intent. These agreements have the character of arrangements for educational cooperation (student and/or faculty exchanges, joint degree programs, and curriculum development), research cooperation, international development project, and so on. Sometimes these agreements are quite concrete; sometimes they are more an expression of intent. They are made at the department, center, or school, or institutional level. The recent rise of multilateral associations, consortia, and networks in higher education reflects the multilateral character of the process (p. 194).

Partnership Process: Supports and Challenges

Despite the common goals sought by international education partnerships, the processes involved in the development of the collaboration contains unique features and issues. The diversity of the stakeholders in the venture and the context of the educational system in the country contribute to how the partnership forms. The partners bring differing degrees of commitment to the relationship and bring varying levels of resources and expectations. A key step in the partnership process then involves addressing the sometimes contradictory dynamics and ultimately creating a shared sense of understanding. Central to the process is clearly defined expectations. These expectations should address an understanding of each partner's contributions including funding, leadership and governance, and division of benefits produced by the collaboration.

Academic associations, academic consortia, and professional networks have increasingly operated as partners and providers of international education over the last decade (de Wit, 2002), yet "there are a great variety of such academic organizations, and it is not always clear what their objectives and goals are nor how successfully they operate" (p. 193). Therefore, as partners seek mutual understanding, they must take into account all levels of interactions involved in the partnership.

Organizational differences must also be taken into consideration. How might the contributions or intentions of the partnership differ for constituents of a two-year versus four-year institution, etc.? What support is available and who are the providers of support within the partnership? Who will champion the partnering process?

Supports for Partnerships. Heffernan and Poole (2005) created a list of practices essential to successful international partnerships, including communicating guidelines and timeframes; cross-cultural awareness training; building trust through competency, contracts, and face-to-face interactions as much as possible; and demonstrating internal and external commitment. This framework can help support the burgeoning development of an international partnership. Several important factors contribute to partnership success (de Wit, 2002), not the least of which is building strong relationships that will last long term. How existing inventory and cultivated resources are employed also bolsters new partnerships. Having limited and achievable goals that build on the experiences of stakeholders' interest produces a stronger foundation and moves beyond short-term thinking or quick fixes. A danger present is the pull to do too many things at once and not recognizing discrepancies in partner needs or attending to potential tensions. A champion of the partnership is a key linchpin to the process whose oversight of these practices contributes to the health of the partnership.

In the case of a partnership between the College of Education at Minnesota State University and Northern International University in Magadan, Russia, the creation of an International Programs Advisory Committee (IPAC) served the champion role (Zahn, Sandell, and Lindsay, 2007). This committee pulled together key players in the partnership process and was charged with overseeing funding and data collection of study abroad programs to help create buy-in among faculty and staff, expand their global presence, and increase partnerships with international institutions.

Governmental offices also serve as important advocates for international partnerships and aid in the partnership process. In 2007, the Spanish Ministry of Education streamlined its higher education admission process by accepting the Chinese university-entrance qualifications. This partnership coincided with efforts to recruit more international students from China, a country where business enterprise is expanding (Labi, 2009). The role of champion for a partnership occurs at many levels, but with the ultimate purpose of supporting the collaboration and obtaining shared outcomes.

When investigating what partnerships have worked for other institutions, it is important to ask the following questions: How did these partnerships overcome challenges? What are some of the lessons learned? What are some of the best practices? What will work for our culture? What will work for our partner's culture? Understanding the answers to these questions can help improve future partnership developments.

Challenges to Partnerships. With any partnership there are bound to be some challenges faced along the way, particularly among mandated partnerships or in situations of divided loyalties. What makes these partnerships fail? According to Tedrow and Mabokela (2007), for successful partnerships to develop, it is important to deal with conflicting group identities, incompatible views, power struggles, funding disagreements, unclear contractual agreements, differing academic calendars, confusing partnership roles, differing values in leadership, and cultural differences. Research identifies several types of challenges that serve to undermine partnerships including cultural differences, communication breakdown, lack of trust, and lack of commitment (Heffernan and Poole, 2005; Tedrow and Mabokela, 2007). Not all members may share the same organizational, institutional or national culture, beliefs or values. For example, a consortium of research universities, the U21 Global, recently announced damaging financial losses and withdrawal of affiliate universities, due to lack of curricular quality assurance and faculty participation, diverging educational standards among the multiple participating nations, and the high cost of distance education (Kolowich, 2009).

Challenges can also evolve from political strategies and policies executed as partnerships form. Creating policies requires the use of power and authority, which often leads to conflict (Tye and Tye, 1992). The unequal basis of power in a partnership and the ways in which power is wielded can have detrimental impacts for all constituents, and threaten the sustainability of the relationship. Abusive use of power can manifest itself in different forms, such as coercion, authority, economic dominance, forceful persuasion, organizational structures and procedures that favor privileged partners, or through restrictive communication tactics (Fowler, 2009). Unequal distribution of dominance is a particular area of concern for partnerships involving developing countries, where power is already limited by lack of resources.

In addition to overcoming conflict, partnerships also face demands to assure measurable performance outcomes. Contributing to the difficult task of quality assurance are contested differences among partners around cultural, organizational, and institutional differences that make it difficult to assess quality due to divergent views and definitions of quality, performance indicators, and peer reviews (Hodson and Thomas, 2001). To address some of these issues, the Australian government established the Australian Universities Quality Agency (AUQA) to oversee quality audits of all Australian institutions of higher education (Woodhouse, 2006). The agency has signed agreements with councils in partnering countries to help gather data to assure quality enforcement of programs (e.g., the Higher Education Quality Council–South Africa, New Zealand Universities Academic Audit Unit, Hong Kong Council for Academic Accreditation, and the National Assessment and Accreditation Council–India).

To circumvent some of the challenges inherent in international education partnerships, it is important to answer some critical questions. What are the available resources and who controls them? How will partner needs and objectives be met? Do all parties have the capabilities to support this partnering model? Is the partnership cost effective? Efforts for collaboration are likely to fail without the establishment of a strong foundation for the partnership.

Conclusion

Institutions of higher education must look beyond their borders to maintain viability in an increasingly competitive yet collaborative world, and perhaps the best answer is through international education partnership. Once institutions have identified key stakeholders, constituents, and attractive forms for partnership, it is essential that partners examine and undergird supportive efforts to combat potential challenges or mitigating circumstances that may affect the sustainability of the partnership. In particular, institutional leaders must allocate time and resources to building and maintaining partnerships, establish institutional processes to nurture a culture of internationalization, and create measures of accountability to assess the health of partnerships. Finally, institutions should regard international partnerships as core to the internationalization process rather than as a gimmick to attract students or "rock star" international faculty. Only when collaborators are committed to long-term alliance, effective communication, and trust building do partners become invested in the process and outcomes shift from ideation to fulfillment.

References

"About Fulbright." 2009. Retrieved October 28, 2009, from http://us.fulbrightonline.org/about.html

Altbach, P. G. *Comparative Higher Education: Knowledge, the University, and Development.* Greenwich, Conn: Ablex, 1998.

Chapman, D., and Austin, A. *Higher Education in the Developing World: Changing Contexts and Institutional Responses.* Chestnut Hill, Mass.: Center for International Higher Education and the Program in Higher Education, Boston College, 2002.

Crump, M. "College Teams Up with St. Andrews." *The Flat Hat,* December 2, 2008. Retrieved October 28, 2009, from http://flathatnews.com/content/69573/college-teams-st-andrews

de Wit, H. *Internationalization of Higher Education in the United States of America and Europe: A Historical, Comparative, and Conceptual Analysis.* Westport, Conn.: Greenwood Press, 2002.

Eggins, H. "Globalization and Reform: Necessary Conjunctions in Higher Education." In H. Eggins (ed.), *Globalization and Reform in Higher Education.* Berkshire, UK: Open University Press, 2003.

Fowler, F. *Policy Studies for Educational Leaders: An Introduction.* Boston: Pearson, 2009.

Friedman, T. *The World Is Flat.* New York: Picador Press, 2007.

Heffernan, T., and Poole, D. "In Search of 'The Vibe': Creating Effective International Education Partnerships." *Higher Education,* 2005, *50,* 223–245.

Hodson, P., and Thomas, H. "Higher Education as an International Commodity: Ensuring Quality in Partnerships." *Assessment & Evaluation in Higher Education,* 2001, *26*(2), 101–112.

Husén, T. "The Idea of the University: Changing Roles, Current Crisis and Future Challenges." In Z. Morsey and P. G. Altbach (eds.), *Higher Education in an International Perspective.* New York: Garland Publishing, 1996.

Kaye, T., and Rumble, G. "Open Universities: A Comparative Approach." In Z. Morsey and P. G. Altbach (eds.), *Higher Education in an International Perspective.* New York: Garland Publishing, 1996.

Kolowich, S. "Another One Bites the Dust." *Inside Higher Education,* December 2009, pp. 1–2 . Retrieved December 9, 2009, from http://www.insidehighered.com/layout/set/ print/news/2009/12/09/u21

Labi, A. "European Universities Look Overseas for New Partnerships." *Chronicle of Higher Education,* 2009, *56*(4/5), A1–A27.

Mason, R. *Globalising Education: Trends and Practices.* London: Routledge, 1998.

Morey, A. I. "Major Trends Impacting Faculty Roles and Rewards: An International Perspective." In H. Eggins (ed.), *Globalization and Reform in Higher Education.* Berkshire, UK: Open University Press, 2003.

NAFSA: Association of International Educators. *Internationalizing the Campus 2008: Profiles of Success at Colleges and Universities.* York, Pa.: The YGS Group, 2008.

NEW DIRECTIONS FOR HIGHER EDUCATION • DOI: 10.1002/he

Schugurensky, D. "Higher Education Restructuring in the Era of Globalization." In R. Arnove and C. Torres (eds.), *Comparative Education: The Dialectic of the Global and the Local.* Lanham, Md.: Rowan & Littlefield Publishers Inc., 2003.

Shaw, S. "Launching International Collaboration for Interpretive Research." *Sign Language Studies,* 2006, 6(4), 438–453.

Stewart, V., and Kagan, S. "A New World View: Education in a Global Era." *Phi Delta Kappan,* 2005, 87, 241–245.

Taylor, W. "Steering Change in Tertiary Education." In H. Eggins (ed.), *Globalization and Reform in Higher Education.* Berkshire, UK: Open University Press, 2003.

Tedrow, B., and Mabokela, R. "An Analysis of International Partnership Programs: The Case of an Historically Disadvantaged Institution in South Africa." *Higher Education,* 2007, 54, 159–179.

Turner, Y., and Robson, S. *Internationalizing the University.* London: Continuum International Publishing Group, 2008.

Tye, B., and Tye, K. *Global Education: A Study of School Change.* Albany: State University of New York Press, 1992.

"UNH Begins First International Degree Program." *Associated Press,* October 3, 2006.

Woodhouse, D. "The Quality of Transnational Education: A Provider View." *Quality in Higher Education,* 2006, 12(3), 277–281.

Zahn, G., Sandell, E., and Lindsay, C. "Fostering Global-Mindedness in Teacher Preparation." *International Journal of Teaching and Learning in Higher Education,* 2007, 19(3), 331–335.

LEILA TUBBEH is the graduate assistant for study abroad in the Reves Center for International Studies and a master's student in the Educational Policy, Planning, and Leadership—Higher Education Administration program in the School of Education at the College of William & Mary.

JOBILA WILLIAMS is the associate director of academic advising in the College of Arts & Sciences and a doctoral student in the Educational Policy, Planning, and Leadership—Higher Education Administration program in the School of Education at the College of William & Mary.

Part Two

Case Examples

2

Five case examples highlight how Ireland is using collaborations to meet national goals.

Institutional Collaborations in Ireland: Leveraging an Increased International Presence

Pamela L. Eddy

This chapter highlights how shifts in policy within Ireland toward increased global rankings and quality of educational programs and a heightened interest in research have been operationalized on the ground. The Higher Education Authority initiated a Programme for Research in Third-Level Institutions (PRTLI) to provide seed money for research innovation. The research reported here provides an overview of the funding program and showcases five of the funded programs, highlighting how these research collaborations have aided in reaching the goals set in Ireland. Lessons learned include the influential role of the external context, including the Bologna Process and involvement in the European Union (EU), and the unintended impact of pitting institutions against one another. Role transitions from competitor to collaborator were not instantaneous or always long lasting. The role of the champion of the partnership was heightened given the size of the country. Finally, structural features of the funding process worked against sustainability for the partners. Lessons from this research are apparent for partners, faculty members, and policy makers.

Case Studies of Collaboration

The Higher Education Authority (HEA) initiated its Programme for Research in Third Level Institutions (PRTLI) in 1998; to date, four cycles of funding have been awarded, with a fifth cycle of funding proposals started

NEW DIRECTIONS FOR HIGHER EDUCATION, no. 150, Summer 2010 © Wiley Periodicals, Inc.
Published online in Wiley InterScience (www.interscience.wiley.com) • DOI: 10.1002/he.387

in 2009. Delays in the awarding of Cycle 5 funds have occurred due to the budget difficulties facing Ireland. As of mid-2010, award winners had still not been selected. In the first four cycles, a total of €865,273,117 was distributed among 83 funded projects. The HEA emphasized different areas of foci for each of the grant cycles, with increasing emphasis on collaboration and partnerships occurring over time. Programs received one-time funding, with an expectation that they would be self-sustaining when the grant funding ended. Several projects, however, expanded their orientation, scope, partners, and area of coverage in the country and were successful in receiving funding during multiple cycles.

The landscape of postsecondary education in Ireland includes 21 main publicly funded tertiary institutions, seven of them universities and 14 of them institutes of technology (IoT) (Organisation for Economic Co-operation and Development, 2006). Since 2001, the Dublin Institute of Technology (DIT) obtained full degree-granting rights for first masters and doctoral degrees. DIT is the largest of the institutes and differs from other institutes given its age, size, and location, which serves a broad range of educational and technical needs. Some of the universities and IoTs were involved in multiple projects, whereas others were not involved at all. Some universities were well positioned and poised to participate in applications for funding given their established inclusion of a research mission, albeit at a lower level than elsewhere in Europe, whereas other institutions were new to the researching enterprise.

How were the partnerships enacted within the funded research projects? How do partnerships impact changes in research in Ireland? What is the impact on faculty work? What organizational changes result from the partnerships? These are the research questions underpinning this study. Case study methodology was employed to closely examine the interactions among partners and to provide more depth of analysis. The investigation of multiple sites within Ireland allowed for cross-case comparisons. Data collection occurred via case site visits to allow for direct observation of the organizations and participants. Interviews were conducted with key partnership personnel and leaders.

Case sites were purposely selected among the funded projects. First, a range of funded areas was sought to determine the influence of disciplinary orientation on the partnership process. Second, cases were selected that involved a breadth of partners from as few as two to as many as eight. Cases were also selected based on the different types of partnering institutions involved since some included non-third-level organizations. Finally, cases were selected to investigate those most recently funded for the first time in Cycle 4 to those who had received funding over multiple cycles through shifting and expanded projects. The case sites included e-INIS/Cosmogrid (Irish National Infrastructure), the Environmental Change Institute (ECI), the Graduate School of Creative Arts and Media (GradCAM), the Humanities Serving Irish Society (HSIS), and Molecular Medicine Ireland (MMI).

e-INIS/Cosmogrid. Cosmogrid and e-INIS (Irish National Infrastructure) are closely linked projects, with e-INIS (e-INIS—Irish National Infrastructure, n.d.) evolving from the project established by Cosmogrid. Cosmogrid received €11.8 million under PRTLI Cycle 3 to establish a program for research on grid-enabled computational physics of natural phenomena. The lead institution was Dublin Institute for Advanced Studies and partners included Dublin City University, National University of Ireland (NUI) Galway, University College Dublin (UCD), HEAnet, Met Éireann, Armagh Observatory, and Grid Ireland. The initial project supported building a national grid system within the country that took advantage of pooling excess capacity within the technology infrastructure system to deliver uniform and reliable service. The grid provides the technology platform upon which academics and users can take advantage of the power of the computer infrastructure to conduct research. This project brought together users and providers of the infrastructure to take advantage of a pooling of computational resources. In 2006, Cosmogrid published *A White Paper on Irish e-Infrastructure*, which contributed to the argument for funding for e-INIS in Cycle 4. A spin-off of Cosmogrid is ICHEC—Irish Centre for High-End Computing. ICHEC provides space with high-end computing available to researchers and graduate students.

In PRTLI Cycle 4, e-INIS received €12.5 million and included the following partners: Dublin Institute of Advanced Studies, NUI Galway, NUI Maynooth, Trinity College Dublin, and UCD. The goal of e-INIS is to create a federation of electronic infrastructure providers in Ireland, in conjunction with the country's universities. The sharing of resources provides a platform for research that connects all the third-level programs within Ireland and provides a national data service to help coordinate activities. One project utilizing the e-infrastructure is the Digital Humanities Observatory (DHO), a funded project of HSIS. This Web resource serves as an e-resource for the humanities. A Cycle 5 proposal is in the works to help extend the computing infrastructure. The establishment of a group with a common focus for e-infrastructure in Ireland was modeled on best practices in Europe.

Environmental Change Institute. The Environmental Change Institute (ECI) at the NUI, Galway was founded in September 2000 through a commitment of €9.6 million in funding from both private sources and Ireland's Higher Education Authority under Cycle 2 of PRTLI. The ECI is a research center within the Institute for Environmental Studies, a cooperative initiative between the three western Irish seaboard Universities (NUI Galway, University College Cork, and University of Limerick), which together form the Atlantic University Alliance (ECI—Environmental Change Institute, n.d.). Since this initial funding in Cycle 2, NUI Galway has received funding for €1.0 million for a new research program under Cycle 3 as well. The Institute also received funding under Cycle 4 for a total of €11.6 million and worked with the following partners: Cork Institute of Technology, NUI

Maynooth, Trinity College Dublin, University College Cork, and University College Limerick.

The administrators of the institute took a focused approach in the preparation of the Cycle 5 bid. Their proposal centered on climate change and addresses three specific thematic areas. Crossing these main areas were two key capacity building areas—Environmental Research Capacity Development and Informatics, Quantification, and Predictive Capacity Development. As institutional representatives came to the preliminary discussions with varying ideas, the focus was always placed back on the central driving themes. If these themes did not fit with the institutional partner's ideas, they were not included. Constant focusing on the central themes helped drive the discussion, though there were moments of heated dissension in arriving at the final proposal. The alignment of the vision of the two central institutions (NUI Galway and UCC) helped drive the overall process.

Graduate School of Creative Arts and Media. The Graduate School of Creative Arts and Media (GradCAM; GradCam—Graduate School of Creative Arts and Media, n.d.) received €2.1 million in funding through PRTLI Cycle 4 to create a structured Ph.D. program in the area of creative arts and media. There are two named partners for this collaboration: Dublin Institute of Technology (DIT) and the National College of Art and Design (NCAD). Two additional collaborators include the Institute of Art, Design and Technology, Dún Laoghaire (IADT) and the University of Ulster (UU). After funding was announced for GradCAM in fall 2007, a process began to recruit the first doctoral fellows. Eight students began studies in February 2008 and a year later this cohort grew to 15 funded students and four self-funded students. NCAD provided the office location for the collaboration as an in-kind donation, with space available for training seminars, student offices, and meeting space.

Contributing to the success of the partnership was a long history of working together in the area of creative arts. A conference in early 2000 brought the partners together and conversations arose from these meetings regarding advanced degree options, with all institutions realizing that the demand was not great enough for them to go it alone. One of the first initiatives of GradCAM was to create a logo for the new initiative. This symbolized the creation of the partnership and is used on all printed material. Slowly, the concept of GradCAM is growing as a recognized entity in the country. The proposal put forth by GradCAM for Cycle 5 builds on the success of the current funding, namely specific structured Ph.D. programs. In the current proposal, new partners were added on, including an official place for IADT and the addition of UCD to help provide a national platform for the projects. As with other projects seeking funding under Cycle 5, tensions were evident as individual institutions jockeyed for high institutional priority on their own campuses and often were pulled into competition on other bids.

Humanities Serving Irish Society. Humanities Serving Irish Society (HSIS) is a consortium of eight universities (Dublin City University, NUI

Galway, NUI Maynooth, National College of Art and Design, Royal Irish Academy, Trinity College Dublin, University College Cork, and University College Dublin) that was funded under PRTLI Cycle 4 for €28.9 million. Of note, each of the participating universities rated HSIS as a top priority in their letters of support during the funding evaluation. Furthermore, previous PRTLI funding cycles had not supported humanities-based research partnerships, thus the HEA review panel was inclined to support HSIS. The Royal Irish Academy (RIA) serves as a neutral convener for the various humanities research projects and the HSIS Web site showcases the range of research underway. The RIA published a monograph titled *Advancing Humanities and Social Science Research in Ireland*. The paper served as the foundation argument for the creation of HSIS under Cycle 4. The HSIS acts as an umbrella group with research clusters among institutions under this structure. A precursor to HSIS was the creation of the Moore Institute at NUI Galway.

The main collaboration effort of HSIS is the Digital Humanities Observatory (DHO). This project involves the creation of a Web-based humanities resource. This project entails the storage and preservation of digital sources in the humanities, with access available to a wide range of users. DHO is supported by the e-infrastructure developed by the Cosmogrid program outlined above.

"The DHO will work to ensure a set of common standards based on best international practice to enable the fullest exploitation of existing national research collections and data repositories. In doing so, the DHO will be filling a critical gap in Ireland's humanities research infrastructure, as identified by a wide range of policy documents and reviews including the Academy's report: Advancing Humanities and Social Science Research in Ireland. The DHO will also incorporate a strong teaching and learning aspect by contributing seminars to a HSIS bi-semestrial postgraduate seminar series as well as organizing its own annual standards seminars and technical workshops" (HSIS—Humanities Serving Irish Society, n.d.). A PRTLI Cycle 5 proposal was put forth with NUI Maynooth as the lead institution. The proposal is for a structured Ph.D. program in the humanities with a focus on digital process. Like other partnerships in Cycle 5, HSIS was split by the tensions among member institutions. In the end, University College Dublin pulled out of the collaboration and put forth its own proposal.

Molecular Medicine of Ireland. Molecular Medicine of Ireland (MMI) is a "not for profit company established [in 2007] by the National University of Ireland Galway, the Royal College of Surgeons in Ireland, Trinity College Dublin, University College Cork, and University College Dublin to coordinate their biomedical research and education activities" (MMI—Molecular Medicine of Ireland, n.d.). MMI received funding to aid in its establishment under PRTLI Cycle 4. In addition to the founding of the national organization, the funding under Cycle 4 supported a Clinician Scientist Fellowship Programme involving all partnering universities; €11.2 million was awarded.

MMI is built upon the foundation established by Dublin Molecular Medicine Centre (DMMC). DMMC was established in 2002 as a partnership among Trinity College Dublin, University College Dublin, the Royal College of Surgeons, and their associated hospitals. This collaboration received €44.8 million under PRTLI Cycle 3 for the creation of the Programme for Human Genomics. Tracing further back, the genesis of DMMC is rooted in funding under PRTLI Cycle 2 when a total of €26 million was awarded to UCD and TCD to establish a partnership to bring together key researchers in the country to pool resources and expertise for the study of molecular medicine.

The evolution of the study of molecular medicine from a regional focus in Dublin to the current national collaboration highlights the push for collaborations in Ireland. The critical mass of expertise among the partners provides leverage to accomplish more than any single institution could do on its own. A tension exists, however, in the current partnership since the Royal College of Surgeons in Ireland opted not to participate in the PRTLI Cycle 5 proposal put forth by MMI. Instead, the RCSI put in a competing bid for funding with other partnering institutions. A clear dilemma of dual loyalties to the MMI collaborative and to institutional priorities was evident. NUI Galway took the lead on the Cycle 5 proposal for MMI. What remains unknown is how the opting out of the Cycle 5 funding bid by RCSI will impact the overall objectives of MMI or how this larger collaboration will adjust. The RCSI is still involved in the Clinician Scientist Programme under Cycle 4 and this project continues until 2010.

Findings

The national goals for higher education in Ireland are linked to Ireland's National Development Plan (NDP), 2007–2013—Transforming Ireland (Irish Government, 2009). Education figures prominently into the strategic plan and the Higher Education Authority (HEA) has incorporated the national goals and objectives into their own plans. The focus for the tertiary education system centers on increasing access to higher education, increasing Ph.D. students within the country, and increasing institutional prominence within the EU. The NDP underscores the need for collaborations to achieve the goals outlined, thus tertiary institutions in Ireland are motivated to partner in attempts to meet national goals. Supporting this platform for collaboration is the HEA funding in PRTLI, which increased its emphasis on the role of partnering to obtain grant monies.

The research conducted on the case sites identified above found four key findings. First, the type of motivation for partnering contributed to the alignment of values and mission among partners. Those with similar value structures and mission beliefs were able to weather storms of conflict because there was a basis for the collaboration beyond funding. For some of the cases, it was a matter of convenient alliances, whereas for others there was shared interest in obtaining a common outcome from the collaboration. Second, the role of an internal champion for the partnership made a difference. The amount of social capital possessed by the champion contributed to how quickly the partnership formed and how well it operated. Third, the partnerships had impacts on individual institutional operations and ultimately on faculty work. Policies were created to deal with the newly formed collaborative entities, some of which impacted individual campus policies as well. For the most part, the work done within the partnership was added to faculty obligations, most often without any additional compensation or acknowledgment from within the institution. Finally, the external context influenced outcomes. Ireland is nested within several larger systems that contribute to internal policy and outcomes. For instance, as a member of the EU, practices in this larger entity influence the norms within the country, particularly in the sciences. Participation in the EU also increases the potential partners available to faculty and universities that may supersede partnerships possible within the country.

Motivation and Value Alignment. Various motivations contribute to how partnerships were formed, how they operated, and how they were held together. Clearly, the availability of extra funding was a motivator for all the partnerships. The infusion of funding to support collaborative research and to create doctoral programs was a new phenomenon in the country. Each college had to rate the proposals put forward to the HEA, basing their priorities on the internal needs and missions of the individual institutions and the alignment with the request for funding programs by the HEA.

In two of the cases outlined above, groups had published white papers that reviewed the state of programming and research needs within the discipline. This preparatory work laid a firm foundation for arguments they put forth in their funding proposals and added a sense of legitimacy to the partnership. HSIS and Cosmogrid both built their proposals on the findings of the needs assessments the partners conducted for the white papers to show the rationale for the projects. The white paper served to bring the group together and began to create a sense of a shared understanding of goals for the collaborators.

The size of the country meant that the faculty members working on areas of common research were known to one another and that the faculty may have had previous working relationships through funding received within the EU or through one of the EU science foundations. Likewise, partners may have worked together in hosting a conference or previous smaller collaborations. The social network in the country made it possible to readily identify potential partners, but the shift from competitors to collaborators was not always smooth. The pull of loyalty to one's home institution and supporting the vision and goals of the college often ran counter to shared partnership projects. Value alignment often was high for those partnerships built in the disciplinary margins, such as the creative arts and in the humanities because alternative funding sources were limited. Areas in the sciences, on the other hand, had more options because there was funding through the science foundations and within the EU and the ability to partner with others outside the country. Also, faculty in the sciences had longer experience with grant-funding and the process of applying for funding.

Role of the Champion. The champion of the collaborative effort served as the initiator for the group, bringing together partners from around the country. This person also set the tone for the type of interactions that occurred among the partners, often negotiating conflict and serving as a final arbitrator in decision-making. Some institutions had reputations of working well together, whereas others were viewed as rogue partners merely following the money and having less altruistic reasons for participating.

The champions within the partnerships often had large levels of social capital accrued (Coleman, 1988). Social capital refers to the ability of individuals to leverage influence in relationships based on the strength and closeness of these relationships, the amount of trust established between players, and the intensity of these relationships relative to their importance to each other, the institution, and the partnership. Ireland is a small country, thus personal relationships with others in similar fields were common and often of long duration. Strong champions were able to use their influence to bring players together, but also were able to keep the peace when conflict arose. It was easy to be a champion when money was readily available, but less so when it was not. Those with higher levels of social capital navigated the lean times better.

Contributing to the relationship building was the labor market patterns within the country—faculty members and administrators exhibit less mobility than counterparts located in the United States. Generally, when a faculty member started their career in one institution, they stayed at this institution. This pattern often influenced loyalty to the institution over partners when disagreements emerged.

Impact on Organizations and Faculty Work. The partnerships created new entities and infrastructures; as a result, policies emerged as the collaboration developed. A project manager was identified for each of the funded projects and each manager often received either part or all of his or her salary from the funding or from in-kind support by one of the institutions. Funding also supported administrative staff for the newly formed partnership. Generally, a board was created to provide support for the project manager and consisted of representatives of each of the colleges or organizations involved. The individual members held allegiance to the partnership, but also to their home institution. As project polices were created, each institution had to react to ensure a meshing of the overarching policy with internal procedures.

Faculty members were involved in a number of different capacities. For instance, faculty members were assigned as supervisors within newly created Ph.D. programs. This supervision and leading of topic workshops or classes typically came on top of the faculty members' institutional assignment. It was unclear how this faculty work was valued within the tenure and promotion cycle.

External Context Influences Outcomes. Prior to the availability of funding within Ireland, the majority of grant monies came from awards within the EU. The awards were most often through EU-sponsored programs or through specific science foundation grants. Participants noted that one of the benefits of the HEA funding was that it did not have onerous reporting requirements. It was often unclear to the partners, however, how the reports they filed were used by the HEA. Partners were quick to state that if the difficulty of reporting increased, the benefit of seeking funds would decrease and that EU funding would be sought instead.

Not only did the partners collaborate with others within Ireland, they also worked with researchers and scholars throughout the EU. The structure of these outside collaborations influenced perceptions of how Ireland should be working. One partner who was familiar with the processes in the United Kingdom (UK) noted his perception of differences among collaborations in Ireland relative to the UK. He related that when funding shrank in the UK, there was a tighter bonding of the partners to one another and a focus on the partnership, whereas in Ireland, when funding decreased, partners were viewed as competitors and the tendency was for individual institutions to seek opportunities that benefited the individual college rather than the partnership.

Lessons Learned

Partnerships among higher education institutions in Ireland, and the success of these collaborations, were dependent on the voice of the champion. The amount of clout and influence that the champion possessed mattered in terms of who was at the table for conversations, the resources available, and the longevity of the group project. Champions with high levels of respect in the field and good relationship-based skills were the most successful. When the champion led the group to create common goals and a shared vision, the partnership was stronger. For example, INIS built on the success of Cosmogrid and sought to develop the technical infrastructure within the country. This focused goal helped shepherd the group through multiple funding opportunities both by the HEA and within the EU. The partnership focus did shift from its initial work with faculty working on the grid to more focus on the process of the infrastructure, but the strong overarching goals reinforced by the champion helped to weather these shifts.

Areas of struggle were evident in proposal creation for PRTLI Cycle 5. During the preparation of proposals, several partnerships were strained by competing demands of individual partners that were tied to shifts in institutional mission or to the belief that the college could do a better job of going it alone or by initiating a competing partnership proposal. How these tensions were handled dictated the outcomes for the existing partnership.

NEW DIRECTIONS FOR HIGHER EDUCATION • DOI: 10.1002/he

The ECI was quite clear on its priorities and created a conceptual map to illustrate this work. When conversations veered from these common goals, potential and continuing partners were reminded of the ultimate outcome and told that their contributions needed to align with this shared view. Partners with other goals were not included in the proposal. Previous work with partners created a history of knowing who could work well in the group, who could follow through on deadlines and promises, and who could be productive collaborators.

Previous interactions among the partners served as a foundation for current partnerships, underscoring that history together matters. As outlined in the cases above, white papers and position briefs often served as the foundation for funded programs. The time invested in creating the white papers also afforded partners an opportunity to get to know one another and to build trust. The small size of the country enables a fertile ground to create relationships, but the downside is that memories of bad partnerships are long-standing and difficult to overcome. Of interest, during the timing of Cycle 5 calls for proposals, Trinity College Dublin and University College Dublin announced the creation of an innovation corridor. This unique arrangement was perceived as a sidebar deal that might undercut ongoing partnership relationships and threaten new proposals.

The current period of financial exigency means that pressure is mounting for partners to obtain funding. Now, the role of the champion becomes more critical, as do past successes of partnership outcomes. The tendencies in the partnerships were attempts to predict outcomes and to calculate the probability of success by partnering with one institution over another. This type of risk assessment meant that some partners were focused on obtaining the best deal versus on the project vision per se. The gains for some partners were solidified and commitment reinforced because resources were tight.

By far, the biggest conclusion of this research was the success of the HEA in increasing research efforts and collaboration among tertiary sites in a scant ten years of funding (Higher Education Authority, 2008). The HEA leveraged change through its requirements for funding, namely the requirement to collaborate with other institutions of higher education so as not to duplicate services. Knowing the influence of policy and funding on obtaining change can establish intentionality in how RFPs are used to influence policy.

The demise of the Celtic Tiger, the term used to describe the rapid expansion of the Irish economy between 1995 and 2007, leaves much unknown about the future. The decline of resources created uncertainty among partners and within the country. Can the larger goals of increasing reputation and prestige of Ireland's colleges be sustained in the current economic climate? The research reported here helps to emphasize components to successful partnerships, namely having a strong champion, shared goals, and interaction among partners to build trust. The HEA-funded partnerships reviewed in this research showcase how the projects have helped to increase research within the country through collaboration and also to increase the number of advanced trained Ph.D. students who will be able to carry on research in the future as well. Faculty worked within the partnerships to help support both research endeavors and supervision for Ph.D. students. What remains unknown is how this level of involvement will be sustained given the lack of a corresponding reward structure for this faculty work.

Changes to institutional policies will help codify how faculty are rewarded, as well as provide evidence that the partnerships are important to the individual colleges and have more chance for sustainability. Training team members on ways to address conflict and how to manage group dynamics would help in sustainability as well. In the final assessment, Ireland's partnerships among colleges leveraged advancement in achieving the NDP goals of increased international presence and the creation of a stronger infrastructure for higher education in the country.

References

Coleman, J. S. "Social Capital in the Creation of Human Capital." *The American Journal of Sociology,* 1988, *94,* S95–S120.
ECI—Environmental Change Institute. n.d. Official Web site. Retrieved June 15, 2009, from http://www.nuigalway.ie/eci/
e-INIS—The Irish National Infrastructure. n.d. Official Web site. Retrieved June 15, 2009, from http://www.e-inis.ie/
GradCam—Graduate School of Creative Arts and Media. n.d. Official Web site. Retrieved June 15, 2009, from http://www.gradcam.ie/contact.php
Higher Education Authority. *Transformations: How Research Is Changing Ireland.* Dublin: Irish National Infrastructure, 2008.
HSIS—Humanities Serving Irish Society. n.d. Official Web site. Retrieved June 15, 2009, from http://www.hsis.ie/default.asp?DocID=330&RevID=&Tpl=1Template3.asp
Irish Government. *National Development Plan 2007–2013: Transforming Ireland.* Dublin: Government Publications, 2009.
MMI—Molecular Medicine of Ireland. n.d. Official Web site. Retrieved June 15, 2009, from http://www.molecularmedicineireland.ie/home
Organisation for Economic Co-operation and Development (OECD). *Higher Education in Ireland: Reviews of National Policies for Education.* Paris: OECD Publishing, 2006.

PAMELA L. EDDY *is associate professor of Educational Policy, Planning, and Leadership at the College of William and Mary.*

3

A small community college in Ontario, Canada, entered into the international partnership market to offer its programs to a wider audience, supplement college income, and help globalize student learning.

Notes from the Field: Lessons Learned in Building a Framework for an International Collaboration

Dan Holland

Loyalist College is one of twenty-four provincially funded Colleges of Applied Arts and Technology in Ontario. Located in Belleville, Loyalist enjoys one of the smaller student populations in the college system with a full-time student enrollment of approximately three thousand students, compared with the five metro Toronto colleges whose full-time enrollment ranges between twelve and nineteen thousand. With size also come some differences in organizational infrastructure. The large metro colleges have several more layers of administrative positions and support. For example, Seneca College in Toronto is the largest community college in Ontario with a full-time student population in excess of nineteen thousand. Their international office supports over two thousand students from seventy-five countries with twenty-two full-time staff. In comparison, Loyalist College's international office has one part-time staff member who looks after our international student body of nineteen. I currently serve as dean of the Schools of Business and Management Studies, Bioscience and Justice Studies. International partnerships landed on my desk because of the interest from the Chinese market in partnering with business and environmental programs.

Until recently, colleges in Ontario were funded on a competitive growth formula (Ministry of Training Colleges and Universities, 2009). This meant that colleges would receive funding based on how much they grew in relation to the overall growth in the system. For instance, if the system grew by

NEW DIRECTIONS FOR HIGHER EDUCATION, no. 150, Summer 2010 © Wiley Periodicals, Inc.
Published online in Wiley InterScience (www.interscience.wiley.com) • DOI: 10.1002/he.388

31

an average of 5 percent in a particular year, and your college grew by 5 percent as well, you maintained your funding base from the previous year. If instead your institutional enrollment expanded by 7 percent, your college received additional funding because your totals were above the system average. However, if your college only managed to grow by 2 percent whereas the system total was at the higher level of 5 percent, you would lose some of your college base funding, even though you had additional students to teach.

This funding formula put small rural colleges (such as Loyalist) at a decided disadvantage because the competition with large urban colleges for student enrollments created a non-level playing field. Traditionally the majority of the student enrollment at Loyalist had homes in the rural region surrounding the college. Research indicates that a rural location influences operations at colleges in remote areas, including impacts on student enrollments (Eddy and Murray, 2007). Given these economic realities, college leaders began exploring other revenue-generating initiatives to offset the slip in government funding and the shifting demographics of the region. The growing interest in international collaborations and the burgeoning demand from developing countries targeting postsecondary education resulted in the college pursuing options in the global educational marketplace.

This chapter provides an overview of a college's experience as it explored partnerships within a foreign country. Areas of review include motivations for partnering, challenges, and factors contributing to success. Finally, the chapter presents a student-centered learning model that is at the core of the college's collaborations.

Why China?

As a college leader and principal negotiator for college-based international partnerships, I am often asked the question: Why is Loyalist College in China? Why not India or Mexico or one of any other fifty possible locations? My answer is simple, because China came to us. For many years, the International Office at Loyalist College has consisted of a single staff person responsible for fielding inquiries from foreign students interested in attending the college. This person was responsible for providing information to international students, assisting them with obtaining the proper documentation for permission to study in Canada, and orienting them to the college when they arrived. This structure was successful as the office worked with the limited international students that the college attracted each year.

Early in the millennium, however, college leaders were approached by the owners of York College of Business (YCB), a private two-year college in Toronto, with a proposition that changed the engagement of the college in the international student marketplace. The owners of YCB had strong ties within China and were recruiting students in China to come and study in

Canada. The recruitment activity was not limited to YCB, but also to colleges with whom the YCB had developed agreements. YCB also had a strong network of agents in China who recruited students on their behalf. The for-profit college basically operated as a recruiting agent and received a fee for each student who registered at a particular institution. The YCB saw Loyalist College as an attractive partner for a number of reasons. First, because of the small size of Loyalist, Chinese students would not be overwhelmed in their adjustment to moving to another country and attending college. Second, the low level of student diversity at Loyalist compared with the larger metro colleges meant that Chinese students would be forced to speak English. In the urban colleges, large numbers of ethnic enclaves meant that Chinese students could find comfort in significant populations of others like them and not be pushed to move beyond their comfort zones (Edman and Brazil, 2009).

Limited resources at Loyalist College, both financial and human, made the concept of forming a partnership with a third party who already had an established presence in China very attractive. Our agreement with YCB began with an understanding that they would act as our agents in China to recruit students to come to study at Loyalist College. For this service they would be paid a percentage of the tuition fee generated by the enrollment of Chinese students at Loyalist. To date, however, we have not experienced any significant change in our international student body as a result of this partnership. Attracting students direct from China proved to be a challenge on several fronts. First, the requirement that students acquire a Test of English Foreign Language (TOEFL) score at a minimum of 550 proved difficult. Second, the cost of international tuition ($10,000 CDN) was prohibitive to many students. Third, restrictive government policies in obtaining a Canadian student visa discouraged many students from applying. Fourth, Canadian immigration requires students to provide twelve months of bank statements to prove their financial sufficiency. Other countries such as the United States and Australia require six months and three months, respectively. These reasons all contributed to the fact that the initial recruitment objectives for international students from China never really materialized.

Over time, however, the YCB agents indicated that they had established relationships with some Chinese postsecondary institutions interested in forming a partnership that would expand the role of Loyalist College in delivering programs in China. In 2005, Loyalist College signed a partnership agreement with Zilang Vocational and Technical College located in the city of Nantong in the Jinan Province. Under the agreement, Zilang College was licensed to offer two Loyalist College Diploma programs: Business Administration and Animation. Students enrolled in these programs would be given the option to study two years at Zilang College and if they qualified would be able to take the third year of the program at Loyalist College. For students to qualify for the third year at Loyalist, they must reach the TOEFL score of 550 and be eligible to apply for a student visa.

NEW DIRECTIONS FOR HIGHER EDUCATION • DOI: 10.1002/he

Motivations for Partnering

The demand for college education in China is on the increase. The opportunity for Chinese students to enter postsecondary institutions in China is becoming easier as the Chinese government expands the number of both public and private colleges and universities. However, the demand for spots in higher education still far outweighs the supply (Wan, 2006). Estimates indicate that in 2008 just over ten million graduating high school students in China were eligible to write the entrance exams for university. It is expected that some nine million students will actually take the exams. Based on the current number of spaces available in Chinese colleges and universities, a large number of these students (around three million) will not be admitted. As a result, larger numbers of Chinese students are investigating the option to study abroad. Organisation for Economic Co-operation and Development (OECD) statistics indicate that in 2006 approximately 2.9 million students from countries around the world were studying abroad. And this number is projected to grow to approximately eight million by the year 2025 (William and Humphries, 2009). At the present time, the United States attracts the largest single country proportion of these students (20 percent) followed by the United Kingdom (13 percent), France (8 percent), Germany (8 percent), and Australia (7 percent; Sahni, 2009). Canada attracts about 5 percent of international students studying abroad. This 5 percent share equates to about a $6.5 billion business in Canada each year. Of the 178,277 international students in Canada in 2008, China had the largest number (42.54 thousand or 24 percent; Citizenship and Immigration Canada, 2008).

Statistics indicate that following the September 11, 2001, attacks in New York, Washington; D. C., and Pennsylvania, the number of Chinese students flowing to Canada declined from a high of twelve thousand to approximately 7.5 thousand. By 2008, this number had increased again to just over forty-two thousand (Citizenship and Immigration Canada, 2008). In 2008, an estimated four hundred twenty-one thousand Chinese students were studying abroad. Their primary destinations included the United States (23 percent), Japan (19 percent), Australia (12 percent), United Kingdom (12 percent), Germany (6 percent), and other countries (28 percent; Sahni, 2009). These relatively low numbers of Chinese students who select Canada as a destination are due to a combination of high tuition costs, longer visa processing times, and more detailed proof of the ability to pay for their education. Although many Chinese students investigate study-abroad options, many more are choosing "branch campuses" of foreign institutions, out of fear that being away from home for so long will undermine their personal connections at home and make it more difficult to find a job when they return (Laughlin, 2008).

According to Laughlin (2008), "Of all the models for international higher education collaboration with China, the branch campus is undoubtedly the most difficult to implement" (p. 19). Branch campuses of international colleges in China require a Chinese partner, but the degree of partnership varies depending on the individual case. Branch campuses are not created as offshoots of Chinese universities, rather as outreach locales of colleges and universities around the world. Some of the more recognized examples of this type of partnership are the Hopkins-Nanjing Center and the Missouri State University Branch Campus at Liaoning Normal University. Other universities have begun the process of establishing branch campuses, but are waiting for approval from the Chinese government. Colleges and universities in China are tightly controlled by the government and are given quotas on the number of students they can admit in a given year.

In an attempt to avoid the imposed quota system and to provide access to more Chinese students, colleges and universities in China enter into partnership agreements with Western institutions allowing them to deliver programs on their campuses. This concept is different from the branch campus model in that the foreign institution "leases" their curriculum to the Chinese partner, and monitors the delivery of the program. In this operational structure, the Chinese partner is involved in all aspects of the program. They provide the physical space, recruit students and professors, and deliver the curriculum. The foreign institution registers the students into the program, monitors their progress, validates professor credentials, and confers the degree or diploma at graduation. In the case of the partnership between Loyalist College and Zilang College, students will receive a Loyalist College diploma.

The motivation for Loyalist College to get into the business of leasing curriculum to a Chinese partner institution was driven on a number of fronts. First and foremost was the anticipated financial return on a relatively small investment. Typical financial arrangements in these types of agreements are centered on a fee-per-student basis. Entering into an agreement typically involves an understanding regarding the amount per student that will be paid by the Chinese partner. These amounts are often in the $400 CDN to $600 CDN range. Also, in many cases the number of students recruited prior to the program starting is stipulated. Often this number ranges between fifty and one hundred students and will be repeated each year the program runs. Based on this foundation, a typical three-year program would see one hundred students the first year, two hundred in the program's second year, and close to three hundred by year three. Gross revenue to the college would be in the $125,000 CDN to $150,000 CDN range. When you begin to expand your base in China to several partner institutions, the potential revenues begin to make a difference to the college's bottom line.

Agreements also include a provision for students who qualify academically to transfer to Loyalist for the third year of the program. In this case, the institution would collect full foreign student tuition and would pay a recruitment fee to the Chinese agent. A second motivation for Loyalist College to partner in China was the opportunity to slightly modify the makeup of the student body at the college. As a small college in Eastern Ontario, diversity in the student and staff population is minimal. The opportunity to attract larger numbers of Chinese students would provide a learning experience for both our students and our staff, not to mention the potential financial payback from obtaining a larger piece of the international student pie.

These types of partnerships between institutions of higher education in two different countries are usually undertaken through a signed Memorandum of Understanding (MOU), which spells out each of the partnering institutions' responsibilities. The MOU is a generic document used as a basis for negotiation with potential Chinese partners. The basic conditions outlined in the MOU were drafted with the help of our agents at YCB. Because YCB was familiar with establishing partnerships between other Canadian colleges and Chinese institutions, they had a good idea of what the parameters of the agreement should look like. Often these agreements are set up to allow students to transfer to the foreign institution at some point in their program. In the case of Loyalist College, the MOUs often refer to a "2 + 1" or a "3 + 0" option. This means that students who have successfully completed the two years of the program in China can transfer to Loyalist for year three of the program. However, recognizing that not all students would have the financial resources needed to study abroad, the 3 + 0 option allows them to complete the entire program at the Chinese partner institution. However, this type of arrangement comes with some distinct challenges.

Challenges and Solutions

Challenges facing international partnerships revolve around three key resources: money, time, and people. It takes a considerable amount of resources to operate effectively in the international arena, particularly in a country like China. Loyalist was in a position where it possessed few resources in any meaningful size. As a result, the tactic for this partnership was to move slowly, spending a great deal of time getting to know and trust our Chinese agents. In our particular case, this meant developing a working relationship with the YCB group over several years. Initial discussion with YCB started in 2002, but it was not until 2005 that our first MOU was negotiated and signed with Zilang College. Acting as our agent in China, YCB was also working for other institutions, often working on as many as six MOUs with various institutions spread across China. Several draft copies of the MOU floated back and forth between the parties until agreement was reached.

The negotiation period can span months and sometimes years, thus it is important that partnership leaders begin to make live contact with the potential Chinese partner school to begin to build relationships. The building of relationships involves dedicated time and occurs over a long period. And building a trusting relationship extends beyond the boardroom table. An important part of building a sound relationship occurs at meal time.

After long periods of often intense negotiation, breaks are taken to share a meal. In China, both lunch and dinner are orchestrated events, with seating placement of Chinese officials and guests scripted. The highest ranking visitor is seated to the right of the highest ranking Chinese official at the table. The second highest ranking visitor is seated directly across from the second in command from the Chinese institution. Then there is the ceremonial toast to welcome the visitors and offer wishes for a long and prosperous future between the two parties. It is not uncommon for there to be ten to twelve people at the table and each individual is encouraged to offer up to three toasts each towards the partnership. The ability to participate in this type of tradition assists in building the respect and trust of the Chinese partner.

Often during the negotiation stage, the Chinese partner will agree to visit the Western institution. All of this is done partly to see that the potential partner institution is one of quality and can deliver on its promises, but also to show good faith in building a long-term relationship. Basically, building a trusting relationship comes down to both parties doing what they have agreed to in the MOU. Establishing a strong relationship with the Chinese institution prior to signing the MOU will greatly assist in getting the program off to a smooth start. Investing time upfront to ensure both parties fully understand their responsibilities will pay dividends down the road. Recognizing that both institutions are working from a limited resource budget acknowledges that both parties are willing to make sacrifices to make this program a success. In the case of the partnership between Loyalist College and Zilang College, both parties had something the other wanted and both were willing to make concessions to get the deal signed. In the case of Loyalist College, we saw this as an opportunity to move into the Chinese market; therefore, we felt we could be flexible around the fee per student that was being negotiated. In Zilang College's case, they were willing to provide the specialized equipment and software required to successfully deliver the animation program.

Carefully documenting the responsibilities of each institution in the MOU allows for clear and concise communication in the event of any concerns that may arise as the program proceeds. That being said, there are still a lot of details that "get lost in the translation." And that is a key challenge when dealing with Chinese partners. All documentation must be produced and vetted in both languages. Often what you believe is a fairly straightforward statement in English can have a totally different meaning when translated into Chinese, and vice versa. A considerable amount of time and energy is spent making sure both parties are reading (and interpreting) the information in the same way. Having a qualified Chinese interpreter is a must. As well, outlining clearly how the revenue from the program will be collected and shared among the partner institutions is important from the beginning. In the case of the agreement between Loyalist College and Zilang College, payment is clearly outlined in the MOU. The MOU calls for a per-student fee to be paid to Loyalist College for each student registered. All other costs are born by Zilang College. Having a signed MOU allows both institutions to focus on the most important part of the agreement, the students.

Recruiting Students and the English Barrier. For our partnership, the Chinese partner institution is responsible for recruiting students to the program, per the MOU. Students must have a minimal proficiency in English to apply for and be accepted to the program. This entry-level proficiency is administered by either YCB on behalf of Loyalist College or by Loyalist College staff themselves if it happens to coincide with one of the semi-annual visits. Students are also required to take English as a Second Language (ESL) classes in addition to their regular studies each semester. At the end of year two, the MOU allows for up to 30 percent of the students who wish to transfer to Loyalist College for their final year, to do so, provided they obtain a TOEFL score of 550. This is the same score required for any foreign student who might want to apply directly to Loyalist College. Students who remain in China for all three years of the program are required to take all courses in English during their third year. The MOU specifies that the program may be delivered in the first year on a (sixty/forty) split (Chinese/English). In the second year, it changes to an (eighty/twenty) English/Chinese split and by third year it is 100 percent English delivery.

Recruiting Qualified Professors. Perhaps one of the biggest challenges to a small institution like Loyalist is that budget limitations mean that the college cannot send its own faculty to teach the course abroad, rather we must rely on our Chinese partners to recruit qualified professors. Generally speaking, it is relatively easy to find qualified ESL teachers, as the number of retired teachers from Western institutions who want to experience China on a contractual basis has increased. The challenge lies in finding qualified professors in the subject area needed, in our case both business and animation teachers. The MOU specifies that we will assist in recruiting Western teachers for the program. The students have made it clear that they want to learn from Western teachers. This requirement has proven more difficult than originally anticipated. Qualified teachers in specific fields such as Animation or Human Resource Development are not readily available.

To try to live up to this part of the agreement, we have expanded our agreement with our partners at YCB asking that they assist us in recruiting qualified Western teachers for the program. When Western teachers cannot be found, courses are taught by qualified Chinese teachers and this can result in another barrier. Generally speaking, Chinese teachers have been trained in a traditional Chinese educational model. This model resembles the traditional architecture of Western educational institutions, which is a distinctive role-bound teacher-led model. But the late 1980s and early 1990s saw a major reform movement take place in Western education that placed the learner first. Attempting to describe to Chinese-trained professors that the student should be placed first and professors become facilitators in the classroom is an extremely difficult concept for them to understand, let alone

NEW DIRECTIONS FOR HIGHER EDUCATION • DOI: 10.1002/he

embrace. To overcome this challenge, discussions have begun to encourage groups of Chinese professors to visit Loyalist College during the May/June period and engage in an intense teacher-training program geared towards a better understanding of how to "facilitate."

Student-Centered Learning Model

In the mid-1990s, many two-year colleges in the West (United States and Canada) began to embrace a new approach to learning. O'Banion (1997) points to a move away from "the time-bound, place-bound, efficiency-bound, and role-bound models that characterized the current day institutions" (p. xiv). Instead, he outlines a new model of education for the two-year community college that he calls "the learning college," an institution designed to help students make passionate connections to learning. Today, many Western-based institutions of higher learning (Loyalist College included) approach learning from the students' perspective. Whether it is called student-centered, learner-centered, or learning-centered, the emphasis is on the student. In visiting many postsecondary institutions in China, my observations indicate that a more traditional model of learning is still practiced. The professor is the master who conveys knowledge to the students, who then memorize and regurgitate the same information back to the professor. Training the Chinese professors to deliver the course content in such a way as to challenge and engage the students in the process can be very threatening to them. Providing a course outline that does not require a text is equally challenging to the Chinese professor. Without a text the normal form of evaluation often does not fit. Professors are not able to assess students strictly on "content" and therefore must understand and implement other measures of student performance such as journals, portfolios, and peer evaluations.

Evaluation of student learning is a critical component of the student-centered learning model. The MOU allows for complete disclosure of the students' progress to Loyalist College and for a minimum of two on-site visits per year by the institution. Depending on the size of the program, this can be challenging if things start to get off the rails. Again, however, this comes down to the restriction of time and resources that can be allocated to the partnership. Typically, the data that is collected includes student transcripts, copies of students' work, course evaluation tools and rubrics, and journals of conversations between the students and the college representative. Longitudinal evaluation of student learning will contribute to program changes and partnership requirements.

Lessons Learned

Our partnership ventures in China taught us many lessons that others might note as they begin joint international ventures. First, depending on the size and scope of your institution's international operation, you will need support from several levels inside the college. Support from senior-level administration is critical. International activity needs to be seen as contributing to the strategic goals and direction of the institution. This can be from a strictly revenue enhancement perspective or an increased campus diversity perspective or a combination of both. If support from the highest level of the institution is not there from the start, the project will have a difficult start and trouble sustaining itself because these partnerships often take several years to develop and pay back dividends to the college.

Second, if you are a small college, like Loyalist, with minimal resources to put into this type of venture, you need to find someone who has an established network within China, who can assist in finding suitable and interested partners in China. By utilizing the services of an "agent" you will be able to speed up the process of finding compatible partner institutions in China. If not, you may end up knocking on a lot of doors with very little success and the time needed to do this will be at the expense of your regular day-to-day responsibilities.

A third lesson I learned has to do with preparing for your first visit to China. China is a nation of deep cultural heritage and the Chinese respect and celebrate their heritage in an open and expressive way. Before going to China, it is important to gain an understanding of Chinese history and culture. A short course in basic Mandarin language and the proper conduct expected during meetings and social gatherings in China can be beneficial. Something as simple as exchanging business cards takes on a whole different meaning in China than it does in the West. Also, critical to your visits to China is a good interpreter. Meetings with Chinese partners are usually long and intense when trying to work out a mutually beneficial agreement. Enlisting the services of a good interpreter is a worthwhile expense.

Further, the Chinese respect strong negotiation techniques from partnering institutions. Also, the evaluation of you as a partner does not stop at the board table, it carries on to the social side of the agenda as well. Following long days around a board table are equally long nights around a dinner table where time is spent getting to know each other on a more personal basis. This includes sharing information about yourself as a person, your family, your hobbies, or other interests. All of this is done as part of relationship and trust building.

Finally, it is sometimes easy to forget that you are in a communist country. Although things may appear to work in a similar fashion to those in the West, they do not. Government control of the education system is real and although many Chinese higher education institutions are enjoying some liberties with respect to partnering with foreign institutions, this all could change with the stroke of a pen from the central educational authority.

NEW DIRECTIONS FOR HIGHER EDUCATION • DOI: 10.1002/he

References

Citizenship and Immigration Canada. *Facts and Figures 2008—Immigration Overview: Permanent and Temporary Residents.* Toronto, Canada: Ministry of Education, 2008.

Eddy, P. L., and Murray, J. (eds.). *Rural Community Colleges: Teaching, Learning, and Leading in the Heartland.* New Directions for Community Colleges, no. 137. San Francisco: Jossey-Bass, 2007.

Edman, J. L., and Brazil, B. "Perceptions of Campus Climate, Academic Efficacy and Academic Success Among Community College Students: An Ethnic Comparison." *Social Psychology of Education: An International Journal,* 2009, 12(3), 371–383.

Laughlin, S. "Trends and Models of Academic Exchange Between China and the U.S." In *Institute of International Education, Global Education Research Reports, Report One.* Sewickley, Pa.: Institute of International Education, 2008, 1–23.

Ministry of Training Colleges and Universities. *2009–10 Technical Document: College Operating Grant Allocations, June 2009.* Toronto, Ontario: Ministry of Training Colleges and Universities, Postsecondary Finance & Information Management Branch, College Finance Unit, 2009.

O'Banion, T. *A Learning College for the 21st Century.* Phoenix, Ariz.: The Oryx Press, 1997.

Sahni, B. S. *Canada's Educational Partnerships Engaging China and India: Selective Parallels, Challenges, and Prospects.* Symposium conducted at the Synergy '09 Education Conference, Toronto, Canada, September 2009.

William, T., and Humphries, J. *Trends in International Student Mobility: Canada/China/India.* Symposium conducted at the Synergy '09 Education Conference, Toronto, Canada, September 2009.

Wan, Y. "Expansion of Chinese Higher Education Since 1998: Its Causes and Outcomes." *Asia Pacific Education Review,* 2006, 7(1), 19–31.

DAN HOLLAND *is dean of the Schools of Business and Management Studies, Bioscience and Justice Studies at Loyalist College, Belleville, Canada.*

4

This chapter illustrates how shared and divergent partner motivations and outcome expectations in a Sino-U.S. cross-border higher education program have created synergy, but also challenged the implementation of a partnership.

International Partnerships: A Game Theory Perspective

Yiyun Jie

Institutions of higher education in China and the United States are increasingly seeking international partners to deliver degree programs to the Chinese populace. This chapter illustrates how shared and divergent partner motivations and outcome expectations in a Chinese cross-border higher education program have created synergy and challenged the implementation of some of these partnerships. A case study of a Sino-U.S. higher education program established by a well-known business school from China and another elite school from the United States is presented to illustrate how such dynamics between partner institutions play out. In particular, game theory is used to highlight the dynamic relationship and nuanced differences between partners' motivations and preferences for expected outcomes.

Background

As illustrated throughout this volume, international organizational arrangements in higher education are by no means a new phenomenon. However, in recent years, the scale and level of economic development derived from internationalization perpetuate the scale of cross-border educational delivery significantly (Garrett and Verbik, 2004). China, in particular, has witnessed rapid growth in the development of cross-border education to the point where it has become one of the leading importing countries of educational programs in the world (Garrett and Verbik, 2004). According to information released from the Chinese Ministry of Education (Ministry of Education China [MOE], 2003a), a total of seven hundred twelve Sino-foreign educational programs/institutions, mostly offering bachelor's degrees or higher, were in place by the end of year 2002. This expansion represents a ninefold increase compared with 1995. About half of the seven hundred twelve programs approved by the MOE are degree-awarding, and almost one-third of all programs are in postsecondary education. The most common areas of study were business administration, enterprise management, accounting, and human resource management. Most of the foreign counterparts are from developed nations such as the United States (one hundred fifty-four joint programs), Australia (one hundred forty-six), and Canada (seventy-four) (MOE, 2003a). These three countries make up two-thirds of the total number of Sino-foreign educational programs or institutions.[1] According to Feng and Gong (as cited in Tang and Nollent, 2007), over thirteen hundred programs operate in China with another three hundred seventy-eight candidate programs at the bachelor's degree level or above currently awaiting approval by the MOE (p. 28).

One of the major problems facing Chinese institutions now is that the dramatic growth in transnational education does not automatically guarantee a desired quality level for every instituted program. Some Sino-foreign educational programs have failed to provide adequate educational resources and services, and some have even illegally or unethically profited through deception and fraud (Sun, 2004; Xinhua Agency, 2004). Because the Chinese government views Sino-foreign educational programs/institutions as an effective means of improving the quality of China's human resources and upgrading the educational system (Zhang, 2003), a series of new policies and initiatives have been implemented to ensure the basic quality of existing and future programs. The Chinese government has established a comprehensive policy framework and administrative monitoring mechanism to ensure that Sino-foreign educational programs/institutions add value to the Chinese education system (MOE, 2003b, 2004a, 2004b, 2004c).

Many discussions and debates have addressed the rationale that drives the dramatic development of cross-border education and the potential benefits it might generate (de Wit, 1995; Knight, 1997, 2005; van der Wende, 1997). A prominent trend has emerged that points to revenue generation as a key lever in increased exportation of transnational programs. At the same time, rationales, such as satisfying unmet demand and educational capacity building are reported more frequently by the importing side of these programs. However, very few empirical studies have looked at both partner institutions' perspectives as rationale for cross-border education with a more balanced approach. As a result, it is unclear whether involved institutions have understood each other's motivations and expectations fully. Furthermore, if partners do hold different expectations for the potential outcomes from the collaboration, how do their different views impact their operation of the program and how do they collaborate while maintaining the balance between competing interests?

New Directions for Higher Education • DOI: 10.1002/he

Game Theory Approach

The purpose of this study is to analyze an international partnership in a cross-border education program through a game theory perspective. Game theory concerns how players interact with each other to obtain their individual goals. It is a particularly powerful tool for understanding and predicting how rational participants behave in a social situation that involves two or more "players" whose interests are interconnected or interdependent (Davis, 1970). In this way, game theory is of direct relevance for this study in terms of interorganizational relations between educational institutions.

A majority of cross-border educational deliveries involve two or more educational institutions from different nations and states in a variety of ways (Davis, Olsen, and Bohm, 2000). Their joint efforts can be perceived as an interorganization cooperative arrangement (Bannerman, Spiller, Yetton, and Davis, 2005; Parkhe, 1993). Involved partners can be perceived as the players participating in a game.

According to game theory (Davis, 1970; Parkhe, 1993; Snidal, 1986), if both players value their own self-interest significantly more than their mutual interest, it is highly likely that they will end up with what is called a prisoners' dilemma situation. This concept means that both partners will forgo some of their most desired outcomes, but only act towards a less-desired outcome because of the risks of being appropriated by the other player. In this situation, the significant discrepancies between how players value the different outcomes have a negative impact on their collaborations because both would avoid choosing the most cooperative strategy. In another scenario, if both partners value their mutual interest much more than their own self-interest, then such discrepancies in their views of the potential outcomes could be addressed through collaboration.

Ultimately, in a collaboration game, the more partners value shared outcomes over self-interest, the more likely the collaborative program will be sustained and continue to be successful. When self-interest evolves over time and becomes equally important and/or outweighs the common interest, sustaining and implementing the partnership is challenged. Thus, new negotiations are needed. If partners have only mutual interest but no self-interest, then it is a pure coordination game. In such a situation, partners share the same value for the potential outcomes and do not have any self-interest and therefore only want to cooperate with each other to achieve that outcome.

Child and Faulkner (1998) suggest that partners often have both similar and different goals and expectations that ultimately influence their actions. Although collaborations presumably serve the interests of both partners in cross-border higher education programs, some evidence suggests that partners may enter these arrangements with quite different motives and expectations. With often ineffective trust, commitment, and communication across partnerships, discrepancies among partner motivations, goals, and expectations are not clearly understood and transparent (Borys and

Jemison, 1989; Child and Faulkner, 1998). When different expectations do exist, how do they impact the partner institutions' collaboration in the operation of the program?

The establishment of a cross-border partnership implies that institutions, based on their own particular interests, have rationalized potential outcomes and accordingly agree to act towards a common outcome. Game theorists call this situation an equilibrium outcome. However, the stability of such an equilibrium outcome, in this study the collaborative program, depends on whether it continues to generate the most mutually preferred outcomes for both players and whether there are other self-interests that are worth the player's unilateral defective actions.

This study examines both discrepancies and similarities between partner institutions' motivations, perceptions of expected outcomes, and desired strategies to achieve such outcomes in cross-border higher education programs. It also evaluates the potential impact these discrepancies and similarities could have on the programmatic level of cross-border educational programs, in the context of mainland China (hereafter referred to as China).

Project Background

A case study of a Sino-U.S. higher education program, established between two elite business schools in China and the United States, is presented to illustrate how such dynamics between partner institutions play out in a cross-border higher education program. This study employed document analysis, site visits to each of the schools, and 13 one-on-one semi-structured interviews (six in the United States and seven in China). Obtaining data from different sources provided a more comprehensive and holistic picture of the case and helped to triangulate the findings (Denzin and Lincoln, 2005). Relevant documents included each institution's mission statement, strategic planning documents, a collaboration agreement, advertisements, course schedules, and evaluation results. The content analysis of these documents helped identify the institutional profile, uncover the values of cross-border education, learn about partner institutional cultural and academic contexts, and identify the administration and curriculum structure of the joint program.

In the in-depth interviews, I asked open-ended questions about participants' perceptions of the rationale that their home institutions had related to being involved with the target program. I also asked questions about the priority over benefits and program outcomes and their understanding of their partner's priorities. Finally, I explored the challenges in providing the programs, and strategies to sustain and enlarge the gains.

Case Descriptions

The Garden EMBA (GEMBA) Program is a Sino-U.S. Executive Master of Business Administration (EMBA) program delivered in southeast China, jointly offered by Prancellion Business School (PBS), a school at an American university, and Yu-Cai College (YCC) housed at a Chinese university (note pseudonyms are used for the names of the colleges). Both partners' home institutions are elite universities in their own countries. Prancellion is a top 20 U.S. business school at a public research-oriented university in the Midwest of the United States, and Yu-Cai College, affiliated with one of the "985 Project" flagship universities in southern China, is a top business school with traditionally wide international connections.

The Garden EMBA Program was inaugurated in 2001, after a three-year period of partner selection and negotiations, including gaining accreditation and approval both from China and from the United States. The program offers 16 EMBA English-taught courses over 16 months for a total of 48 credits, including a two-week international residency in the United States. Courses are delivered on two consecutive weekends each month. Every course is co-taught by two faculty members, one from Prancellion School and one from Yu-Cai College, and facilitated by a doctoral graduate student or junior faculty member from Yu-Cai College. As graduation nears, Garden EMBA students work with EMBA students enrolled in Prancellion School's other global EMBA programs on a half-year "virtual team project." By graduation, Garden EMBA students complete their two-week integrated international residency in the United States, and graduate with an MBA degree from the American university.

As one of the earliest joint EMBA programs established in China in 2001, the Garden Program has successfully built a reputation in the local region of southern China. On four different occasions, the joint venture has been ranked by the China EMBA Forum as the number one joint EMBA program in China based on the program's market reputation, evaluation by graduates, and program features. The program successfully overcame numerous difficulties and has been able to sustain itself over time. The Garden Program is now self-sustaining with a small but steady enrollment, and is a well-recognized EMBA program in the local region.

To understand the partners' motivations and perspectives on the expected outcomes of the joint program, it is important to understand the unique institutional features of the colleges in regard to internationalization. With the mission "to develop tomorrow's top business leaders," the Prancellion School from the American university is fully committed to delivering a global experience to its students. The U.S. school has student exchange relations with 20 countries; three Joint Executive MBA degree programs on two continents; and 10 short-term global enrichment elective partnerships. It also has alumni residing in 78 countries around the world. With such strong global connections, Prancellion has established distinct features in the area of internationalization. More recently, the home university of Prancellion has launched comprehensive strategic plans for internationalization of the entire campus, aspiring to become one of the top research-oriented universities in the world. As one of the leading colleges promoting internationalization strategies at its home university, Prancellion School has introduced an international experience requirement for all its undergraduates.

NEW DIRECTIONS FOR HIGHER EDUCATION • DOI: 10.1002/he

Yu-Cai College in China has a unique history in regards to internationalization because it was originally a missionary university established by Americans in the 1930s. The school was integrated into a Chinese comprehensive university in the 1950s; however, the identity of Yu-Cai College was strongly sustained among alumni and well-recognized in the local region. The commitment from some of the successful alumni, who now live in Hong Kong and overseas, is so strong that they actually fund and oversee the current development of Yu-Cai College through the Board of Trustees. The Board of Trustees has always been the advocator for internationalization of Yu-Cai College, directing it to become more internationally oriented.

Findings

A number of diverse reasons motivate the two partner institutions and the colleges to seek institutionally desired outcomes. Nevertheless, the partners also have a range of similar and some different interests in the overall expected outcomes for the joint program. These individual motivations and outcomes include enhancing the brand influences and prestige of the home institution, generating reasonable revenue, and providing learning opportunities for faculty and students. Moreover, although in the early development stage, partners had high congruency in terms of motivations and similar outcome preferences, namely to establish a high-quality self-sustainable EMBA program with a good brand image in southeast China.

A collaboration game situation was identified in the partnership, particularly in the early development stage. However, now that the program is in the development and expansion stage, different outcome preferences between partners have emerged and challenge the program's operation. Partners' views about the priority of different program aspects (e.g., brand influence versus enrollment size) diverge. Although the partners both agree that the Garden Program has been a success, the partners show different interests in its future development. Yu-Cai is interested in ways to better promote the program to a broader region and enhance its level of prestige, while Prancellion is more concerned about the size of enrollment for sustainability. These two preferences do not necessarily conflict and can be complementary; however, they also pull limited program resources in different directions. Such nuanced variation reflects the partners' different expectations for future development of the program in these two aspects. These differences also lead the partner institutions to implement their own preferred strategies, which have triggered misperceptions about the other partner's intent. Nevertheless, the strong sense of trust that Prancellion School and Yu-Cai College have built over their years of collaboration provides solid ground to address these potential issues through productive communication.

Motivations. Expanding brand influence in the local China market is the overriding goal for both Prancellion School and Yu-Cai College. Prancellion School wants to establish their global reputation and network by developing a set of deep partnerships with elite foreign academic institutions in geographic areas that are important to the regional business community, which requires a critical mass of enrolled students. The Garden Program is one of three global EMBA programs offered by Prancellion School in partnership with other leading business universities overseas, so it is an important part of the school's overall strategic plan. These international programs help strengthen the reputation of Prancellion School at the global level, so that it becomes known in other parts of the world. As one PBS interviewee noted, it also helps to create a part of its "brand identity, the international dimension."

Yu-Cai College wants to enhance its brand and prestigious status in China by building its own capacity in Executive MBA education. On the one hand, with its unique history, being internationally connected and recognized is an important aspect of Yu-Cai's identity; on the other hand, because Executive MBA education in China has a very short history compared with the United States, enhancing the college's leading status in economic and business management education cannot be done through collaboration with other Chinese or local universities, but has to be done with elite foreign universities.

Revenue Generation. Both partners recognize revenue-generation as one of the main outcomes. However, making money is not the primary purpose, even though it is a significant influential factor for sustainability of the program. In other words, the joint program has to be self-sustainable so as not to pull over other financial resources from the home institution. Therefore, financially breaking even is the bottom line for both partners. Running the program at a break-even point or close to the break-even point is bearable for both partners, but only for a short period of time.

Faculty Development. Faculty development is another motivation and expected outcome for both partners for the joint program. For Prancellion School, the international programs they established worldwide are expected to provide a wide range of cross-cultural business learning experiences for faculty and students (Sulejewiz, Lesniak-Lebkowska, and Zaidi, 2000). A partnership with an elite Chinese business school has become necessary not only because of China's emerging economy and enormous market potential, but also because of the strong connection that local businesses have developed with China. The program has become a "real-life laboratory" for faculty to experience and learn about one of the world's rapidly emerging economies, as well as to gain a better understanding of the transitioning nature of the Chinese economy. These first-hand experiences and knowledge can be brought back to students on the U.S. campus as faculty members integrate the information into their domestic teaching. For Yu-Cai College, the co-teaching using a teaching assistantship model provides opportunities for Chinese faculty to learn from their foreign collaborators. Junior faculty members at Yu-Cai have been strongly encouraged to participate in at least one Garden Program course before they teach any other domestic MBA courses at the college.

Differences between Partners—A Game Theory Approach

Partners hold different preferences for potential program outcomes. Such preference differences become more explicit as the program expands. At the early stage of the joint program, strategically positioning its brand and representing the home institution worldwide was the most important goal for Prancellion School. Similarly, being able to collaborate with a top U.S. business school and offer an EMBA program with the full American design and instruction is considered to be the most important goal for the Chinese partner. The elite status of both partner institutions and the design of the Garden Program constitute a unique profile for the "high-end" Executive MBA program in China. These unique features include a full English delivery curriculum, a unique "global-local" co-teaching model, multinational mock business collaboration through "virtual team projects," and an international residency in the United States. The fact that Yu-Cai College offers such an education opportunity in China through its international partnership is considered to be an enhancement of its knowledge of development in modern business management education.

For both partners, the expectation for profit generation was not pressing at the beginning. Nevertheless, generating more revenue beyond the break-even point is expected in the long run, especially given the current well-established local brand of the joint program. As the joint program has evolved beyond its initial inception, there is a delicate balance between priorities: the choice between strengthening and continuing to expand its brand image beyond the southeast region of China with the current enrollment size versus concentrating on the local business community to expand a bigger enrollment number. The balance between more efforts in brand promotion or increasing enrollment has become a focal point of current communication between partners. Although having a good brand may attract more prospective students, the two goals (generating revenue versus expanding the global brand) could be conflicting in the short term, as each goal demands a great proportion of the limited program resources.

The joint program illustrates the collaboration game situation in its early stage. Clearly, establishing a high-quality, self-sustainable EMBA program with a good brand image in southeast China was the most preferred outcome for both partners. Their self-interests aligned in this outcome. As the program developed, however, partners' preferences for potential outcomes diverged, because their self-interests led the program in different directions. Ultimately, the different preferences the partner institutions have for brand-building and financial return could jeopardize the implementation strategies the partners want to implement for the program.

For example, although both partners want to provide learning opportunities and experiences for faculty members, the relative importance given to this outcome in regard to brand image differs for the partners. For Yu-Cai

College, its own faculty's direct involvement in the joint program is preferred, but this staffing is secondary to maintaining a high profile for the program. Therefore, as the joint program expands, Yu-Cai College is willing to hire outside faculty members from well-recognized business schools from Hong Kong, Europe, and Shanghai, instead of using its own faculty, even if the latter results in lower costs. In contrast, faculty learning is a key outcome that Prancellion School wants to achieve through the Garden Program; thus, direct involvement of its own faculty members is the key strategy to achieve this outcome. Prancellion faculty represents the school's brand identity as well. There is no evidence suggesting that Prancellion School would consider hiring faculty members from other elite universities in the United States to teach in the Garden Program, even though it may have a big "wow effect" for the program's elite status in the Chinese market, as noted by a Chinese interviewee.

It is still too early to tell how significantly these emerging differences between partners' self-interest would affect the program given that the Garden Program is currently self-sustainable and operating with a relatively steady enrollment number, though not appreciably above the break-even point. Nonetheless, the collaboration game structure still holds strong because self-sufficiency and the high-quality program image are still the goal partners share for the program. Neither of the partner's self-interests would be meaningful if this common ground disappeared. Thus, the pressing issue is how can partners negotiate to achieve the shared outcome given the current situation? Presumably, the branding effect is more beneficial to the Chinese partner and its home institution because the enhanced image of the business school and the university makes the Chinese college's other programs more appealing to potential students locally. Geographic remoteness and other cross-country obstacles make the brand effect less beneficial to Prancellion School in the United States. As a result, the local Chinese partner college is more likely to tolerate a lower net-profit return on the program than the American institution.

Discussion

The key issue to address for a collaboration game is the cooperation between partners to work towards shared interests over their self-interests. Such cooperation requires a great amount of trust. Partners always have some shared interests and some self-interests, but a new round of negotiation is needed when either, both, or one of the partners' preference level changes. Strong trust between partners and open communication about each other's expectations and goals help make the negotiation process more constructive and beneficial for both partners.

Over the years, Prancellion School and Yu-Cai College have developed, sustained, and strengthened their partnership through difficult times. There were times that enrollment in the Garden Program was far below the break-even level, but both partners held on to their shared interests rather than dismantling the program. They successfully overcame these challenges and both demonstrated strong commitment to the partnership that contributed to a strong sense of trust. Thus, the history of the partnership laid solid groundwork for the current stage of the program and its future development. Although sometimes confused by each partner's new initiatives or strategies in program delivery, involved individuals from both schools hold a strong belief about each other's good intentions and have pursued more clarification and communication on pressing issues. This scenario aligns to what game theory describes as a collaboration game. Because the value each collaborator assigns to the shared goal overweighs their self-interests, they can maintain an equilibrium outcome for the game through negotiation and communication.

The lack of a formal and sustainable organizational structure of the collaborative program is one of the emerging issues challenging mutual trust-building. Prompt communication between the partners could be delayed because of this organizational structure issue. For example, because the program is not structured into either partner institution's formal organizational hierarchy, there is limited or no relevant career development path for involved administrative personnel's professional growth. This issue involves both leaders and key administrative staff. As a result, retaining some of the key personnel of the program is an emerging issue. There is frequent turnover of the administrative staff members in the Garden Program office. Because trust between partner institutions is usually carried through and bound within the involved individuals, every key staffing change results in job transition challenges that may lead to miscommunication between partners. If key leadership change in both partner institutions, it is unclear whether the successors will hold the same beliefs and expectations for the partnerships as the former leaders. Every change in these key administrative leaders and staff members affects the sense of trust between the partners. It takes time for people to understand the new situation and rebuild a sense of trust when personnel change in either partners' institutions or the local Garden Program office.

Strategic management theorists have found that a mechanism to increase the frequency of interaction and behavioral transparency would be effective in encouraging collaboration and cooperation (Parkhe, 1993). With the current model setup of the Garden Program, more frequent direct (face-to-face) contact beyond e-mail from both sides of the partnership would be beneficial, despite increases in travel costs. Currently, leaders and key staff from both partners meet in person twice a year, once in November for the opening ceremony of the program and once in May for the graduation ceremony. Setting up regular check-in opportunities and face-to-face contact would help increase both the frequency of interaction and behavioral transparency. Another possible strategy is for Prancellion School to have an on-site representative in the local Garden Program office. This representative could then facilitate more direct and prompt communication between partners.

New Directions for Higher Education • DOI: 10.1002/he

Conclusion

The Garden Program case provides a useful illustration of the collaboration game in cross-border higher education. Although the two partners share similar rhetoric about their motivations and expected outcomes, the subtle differences emerging between their interpretations and preferences regarding different expected outcomes pose challenges to the future of the partnership. It is important to recognize these subtle differences and misperceptions about each other's desired strategies because they could lead the partners to different and potentially conflicting tactics for the existing joint program. Furthermore, without a clear understanding of each other's interpretations around these expected outcomes, partners tend to assume different reasons for their partners' new strategies, proposals, or ideas for further development of the program. Such assumptions may pose a potential threat to the trust between partners, thus challenging the partnership.

Partner institutions should constantly revisit their expectations for collaboration to ensure a shared understanding around potential outcomes and preferred strategies. In doing so, they may find nuance differences between how the partners perceive these shared goals, even if they use similar rhetoric. Leaders and involved staff members should attend to these issues through tactful and open communication, yet be direct and specific.

Note

1. These data are based on earlier information released from the Chinese Ministry of Education. The most up-to-date data on the Sino-foreign education programs in China is still incomplete due to the reevaluation of these programs. Detailed information about the approved programs are released online for the general public.

References

Bannerman, P., Spiller, J., Yetton, P., and Davis, J. *Strategic Alliances in Education and Training Services: A Literature Review.* Canberra: DEST, 2005.

Borys, B., and Jemison, D. B. "Hybrid Arrangements as Strategic Alliances: Theoretical Issues in Organizational Combinations." *The Academy of Management Review*, 1989, 14(2), 234–249.

Child, J., and Faulkner, D. *Strategies of Cooperation: Managing Alliances, Networks, and Joint Ventures.* New York: Oxford University Press, 1998.

Davis, D., Olsen, A., and Bohm, A. "Transnational Education Providers, Partners and Policy: Challenges for Australian Institutions Offshore." Paper presented at the 14th Australian International Education Conference, Brisbane, Australia, October 2000.

Davis, M. D. *Game Theory: A Nontechnical Introduction.* New York, London: Courier Dover Publications, 1970.

Denzin, N. K., and Lincoln, Y. (eds.). *The SAGE Handbook of Qualitative Research.* Thousand Oaks, Calif.: Sage, 2005.

de Wit, H. "Education and Globalization in Europe: Current Trends and Future Developments." *Frontiers: The Interdisciplinary Journal of Study Aborad*, 1995, 1, 28–53.

Garrett, R., and Verbik, L. "Transnational Higher Education: Major Markets and Emerging Trends." In *Mapping Borderless Higher Education: Policy, Markets and Competition*. Oxford, UK: The Observatory on Borderless Higher Education, Alden Group, 2004.

Knight, J. "Internationalisation of Higher Education: A Conceptual Framework." In J. Knight and H. de Wit (eds.), *Internationalisation of Higher Education in Asia Pacific Countries*. Luna Negra, Amsterdam: The European Association for International Education (EAIE), 1997.

Knight, J. "IAU 2005 Internationalization Survey: Preliminary Findings Report." Paris: UNESCO-the International Association of Universities (IAU), 2005.

Ministry of Education China. "Zhongwai Hezuo Banxue Jiben Qingkuang [General information about Sino-foreign joint educational programs]," 2003a. Retrieved February 25, 2006, from http://www.jsj.edu.cn/dongtai/005.html

Ministry of Education China. "Regulations of the People's Republic of China on Chinese-Foreign Cooperation in Running Schools," 2003b. Retrieved May 25, 2006, from http://www.moe.edu.cn/edoas/website18/info6784.htm

Ministry of Education China. "Implementation Measures of Establishing Sino-Foreign Cooperation in the People's Republic of China," 2004a. Retrieved May 25, 2006, from http://www.moe.edu.cn/edoas/website18/info4911.htm

Ministry of Education China. "License Identifier Procedure of Sino-Foreign Cooperation (Interim)," 2004b. Retrieved January 17, 2007, from http://www.moe.edu.cn/edoas/website18/info15141.htm

Ministry of Education China. "Notice of Re-examining Sino-Foreign Educational Institutions and Programs," 2004c. Retrieved January 17, 2007, from http://www.moe.edu.cn/edoas/website18/info6616.htm

Parkhe, A. "Strategic Alliance Structuring: A Game-Theoretical and Transaction Cost Examination of Interfirm Cooperation." *Academy of Management Journal*, 1993, 36(4), 794–829.

Snidal, D. "The Game Theory of International Politics." In K. A. Oye (ed.), *Cooperation Under Anarchy*. Princeton, N.J.: Princeton University Press, 1986.

Sulejewiz, A., Lesniak-Lebkowska, G., and Zaidi, M. A. "Development and Delivery of an American Style MBA Degree Program at the Warsaw School of Economics." In A. Sulejewiz and M. A. Zaidi (eds.), *Polish-American MBA at the Warsaw School of Economics: Lessons Learned from an International Partnership*. Warsaw, Poland: Warsaw School of Economics Press, 2000.

Sun, X. "Future Development of Sino-Foreign Educational Cooperation," 2004. Retrieved February 25, 2006, from http://www.moe.edu.cn/edoas/website18/info5008.htm

Tang, N., and Nollent, A. "UK-China-Hong Kong Trans-national Education Project: Report to British Council." 2007. Retrieved January 3, 2008, from http://www.shu.ac.uk/research/ceir/downloads/TNE%201%20final%20report%20HK%20China%2001-07.pdf

van der Wende, M. "Missing Links: The Relationship between National Policies for Internationalisation and Those for Higher Education in General." In T. Kalvemark and M. van der Wende (eds.), *National Policies for the Internationalisation of Higher Education in Europe*. Stockholm, Sweden: National Agency for Higher Education, 1997.

Xinhua Agency. "The Ministry of Education Will Consolidate Sino-Foreign Educational Cooperation," 2004. Retrieved January 17, 2007, from Factiva, Inc.

Zhang, C. "Transnational Higher Education in China: Why Has the State Encouraged Its Development?" Unpublished monograph, Stanford University, 2003.

YIYUN JIE is a research assistant for first-year experience assessment in the Department of Postsecondary Teaching and Learning and a Ph.D. candidate in the Comparative and International Development Education program in the College of Education and Human Development at the University of Minnesota.

PART THREE

Changing Roles

5

If international partnerships are to be sustained beyond funding cycles and the initial passions of a faculty champion, they need to become institutionalized into the fabric of the department or institution.

Administrative Perspectives on International Partnerships

Marilyn J. Amey

In the race to be internationally present, colleges and universities seek increasing ways to partner across boundaries. Sometimes, arrangements are loose configurations including ways in which individual student or faculty study-abroad activities have traditionally been initiated; sometimes, they are more integrally connected to core institutional mission such as branch campuses. As Sakamoto and Chapman (2010) observe, cross-border collaborations are also moving into research and technology initiatives, institutional capacity building in administration and faculty development, testing, quality assurance, and technology. As these arrangements rapidly expand, single and uniform definitions of benefit and cost are not clear, and they may not actually exist.

Sakamoto and Chapman (2010) argue that we know a fair amount about cross-border instructional arrangements in part because they are a fairly long-standing aspect of higher education. They tend to begin as programmatic initiatives to enhance curricular offerings or are characterized as part of institutional directives to internationalize undergraduate experiences. Noninstructional partnerships may be even more closely aligned with individual faculty scholarly agendas, developed through personal contacts and motivations. Although both kinds of international collaborations are subject to the time and effort of individual faculty members to develop and sustain them, noninstructional partnerships are perhaps even more affected by the role of champions and their funding sources.

Study-abroad programs or faculty exchanges may be more easily built into department or college budgets, and, therefore, provide a more stable

NEW DIRECTIONS FOR HIGHER EDUCATION, no. 150, Summer 2010 © Wiley Periodicals, Inc.
Published online in Wiley InterScience (www.interscience.wiley.com) • DOI: 10.1002/he.390

foundation at least with respect to funding and accounting for faculty members' time. We have documentation of the benefits of study abroad to students (Black and Duhon, 2006; Kitsantas, 2004; Lindsey, 2005; Young, 2003) and can operationalize individual benefits to faculty in noninstructional partnerships in the form of scholarly productivity, for example; how international partnerships measure up when the unit of analysis is a department or college is less clear, and administrative perspectives of these initiatives is less well documented.

Thinking Administratively About International Partnerships

It is possible to examine international partnerships as organizational entities using a multi-stage partnership model (Amey, Eddy, and Ozaki, 2007). The first stage focuses on antecedents, motivation for involvement and the context of the partnership, particularly on the roles of the champion who initiates it. Moving beyond the original motivation that spawns international activity, the second stage of the partnership model focuses on the partnership itself and how it develops (Amey, Eddy, and Ozaki, 2007; Ozaki, Amey, and Watson, 2007). The social and resource capital of individual partners is taken into account in this stage as the relationship evolves. For example, an initiative championed by a full professor with resources to support her work may have more perceived status in a choice set of activities than that of a new assistant professor still trying to negotiate the academic terrain of his department and establishing himself in core work areas. Similarly, in selecting cross-border partners, those who are better able to provide needed institutional status and funding may have greater perceived "worth" than a partner with greater need, but a less stable infrastructure. Stage three of the model examines issues of sustainability and termination. If the international partnership indeed is to be sustained beyond funding cycles and the initial passions of a faculty champion, it needs to become more institutionalized into the fabric of the department or institution. Commitment, understanding, benefits, and costs move from the very local to collective level, from rhetoric of support to actual structural mechanisms through which the partnership activity is maintained. How these shifts to sustainability occur is not always well documented, but that they need to occur if the goal is sustained engagement seems clear (Amey, Eddy, and Campbell, 2010; Amey, Eddy, and Ozaki, 2007).

Organizational development and partnership literature describing innovation adoption in general indicates the importance of how champions and leaders frame initiatives and help others see the mutual benefits of engagement, how partnership activity moves from the fringes of the academic enterprise to a more strategic position in planning processes, and how the outcomes of such initiatives are woven into organizational culture and values (Eddy, 2007; Fairhurst and Sarr, 1996; Fear, Creamer, Pirog, Block, and

Redmond, 2004; Morgan, 1998; Tornatzky and Fleischer, 1990; Weick, 1995; Wolverton, 1998). It is reasonable to assume similar strategies need to occur for international partnerships to transition to the mainstream, as well.

Four international partnerships including both instructional and non-instructional examples are briefly highlighted in this chapter. Short summaries of the collaborations are examined through the lens of the partnership model and focus on administrative and/or faculty issues that arise with the activities, followed by a summary of observations on the specific cases noted here that could be applied to international partnerships in general. Each example is unique in its intent, the ways in which it is evolving, and how it contributes to the life of the department; each began largely under the auspices of an individual's faculty interest; and each provides lessons for partners, faculty members, and administrators.

Exchange Class. This partnership began as an *exchange class* between two adult education programs. Students from each program spent 10 days in each location with a virtual learning component on critical issues in adult education sandwiched in between the site visits. The partner institution had an existing relationship with our college tied to an overseas program for expatriots that was in the process of being closed, and was interested in developing a new, more direct partnership at the program level. At the same time, our graduate program that included adult education wanted to experiment with graduate student international experiences on a small scale. The original plan was brokered by a college staff person quite familiar with international experiences and subsequently led by a champion faculty member. Seven years later, the course has expanded to three sites in the guest country. The curriculum has also expanded to include more general postsecondary issues beyond the specifics of only adult education. Students who have participated speak of this as a "life-altering experience," the unique opportunity for personal growth and self-reflection on cross-cultural issues provided by the group experience, and enthusiastically support its continuance. Although enrollments of students from our department are small (on average, 6–8 per summer), they are manageable for moving around easily in-country and providing for intense and meaningful exchange with students and professionals from the partner institution, whose numbers are comparable. The lead faculty member and several graduate students have engaged in ongoing research on the transformative nature of these experiences.

Challenges we have faced with this exchange class have included, most significantly, the retirement of the college support staff person who facilitated the logistics of the trip and originally brokered the partnership. Our institutional study-abroad system is not set up to easily manage study tour experiences that fall outside the semester and credit system, or that are targeted to graduate students, so logistical support and planning have fallen to the faculty member and department support staff. This has greatly altered the time involved for the faculty and our support staff, as planning, logistics and recruitment constitute almost a course by themselves. In addition, though the program faculty enthusiastically approved the initiative at the onset, it still clearly is seen as the responsibility of the faculty champion. It is still referred to as "Sam's class" and each year, faculty wait for "Sam" to propose the dates, content, and logistics for the course.

Fulbright Outreach. The Fulbright Outreach partnership started as a term-long sabbatical for one faculty member. The work proposed for the term was affiliated with a prestigious inter-country master's program and was also largely deemed an *outreach initiative* for developing innovative graduate programs in-country. Since the actual Fulbright four years ago, the faculty champion has made return visits each year to continue the outreach work. One year ago, visiting scholars from the partner country came to our campus for two weeks during which time they had much interaction with students and other faculty, and explored possibilities of additional cross-institutional collaborations. One off-shoot of this visit was development of a comparative issues in higher education course that will be taught in our program this spring with "in-residence" faculty from the partner country with us for two-week blocks of time; issue-oriented instructional cases based on partner countries are being designed for use in the course as is development of an ability to add international colleague instructors to the course through technology in subsequent offerings of the course. Additional outcomes of the Fulbright Outreach partnership has been the opportunity for another of our faculty to twice visit the country, studying higher education systems there, and hosting a Fulbright scholar from the country this fall who taught a master's policy course for us. What began as an individual's desire to pursue Fulbright funding for outreach work has expanded to include instructional impact on the program back home, as well as potential opportunities for research collaborations on topics of interest between the partner faculty and graduate students. With the development of a comparative class offered as part of our curriculum and the presence of scholars-in-residence, our students see direct benefits from this partnership whether they are personally able to travel internationally or not.

Central issues of this partnering opportunity center on the shift from an accommodation of individual faculty interests in the Fulbright Outreach partnership to involving or benefiting other faculty and students. This is not necessarily atypical with this kind of prestigious award, but when the award occurs during the regular academic year or subsequent time away from campus is requested, other faculty are required to step up and help support the initiative by covering classes, advising students, serving on committees, and so on. How the partnership transcends the interests of the champion or can accommodate similar interests/relationships of faculty with colleagues in other countries is not entirely clear. As department resources get used to support the activities, including sustenance costs for those faculty physically present to teach in the comparative course, it will be interesting to see the extent to which program faculty value this experience as shepherded by the champion or if their support is to a more general idea in which they can all more fully participate.

Professional Development with Students. A different international partnership emanating from another faculty member's year-long Fulbright serves as the third example. Although the sabbatical was over a decade ago, the relationships developed at that time and nurtured during the period since recently formed the basis of an innovative international *professional development* experience for students. Led by the faculty champion, one additional program faculty and a student affairs staff member spent most of spring term developing materials in conjunction with their in-country colleagues to address faculty development needs and assist with the initiation of a new residence hall design. For several weeks during the summer, six graduate students delivered professional development to faculty and student affairs administrators on the ground in-country.

Following the first summer (2007), a contingent of colleagues from the partner country were on our campus during which time a broader network of faculty, students, and staff benefited from in-depth conversation on emerging higher education developments in this international context. A collaborative research project focused on the developing in-country residence hall has begun, as well. A new contingent of graduate students accompanied the same faculty and staff for a return professional development visit in summer, 2009, and a third visit is scheduled for summer 2010. Not only do students describe life-changing effects of the encounters similar in many ways to those experienced by participants in the exchange class, but they also feel much better prepared to engage in international work. Part of the processing of the experience while in-country focuses on issues of cultural context and translation, comparative assessment, and other concepts and skills required to effectively participate in work in different environments. Although not a formal curriculum, the total experience provides a unique opportunity to be involved in authentic professional development delivery while simultaneously engaging in self-reflection and one's own professional growth.

Again, because this experience fell outside the traditional university-supported study-abroad experiences, the logistical work fell to the lead faculty member here and in-country. This involved everything from transport and visa considerations to lodging and funding negotiations. Some of these deliberations were facilitated by the long-standing relationships built by the champion; trying to establish such a program without this social capital would have been almost impossible. Even once the logistics were established making years two and three more readily arranged, there was still the question of financial support for the initiative that needed to be addressed here and in-country. Gaining broader acceptance by the faculty of the priority nature of this experience to release department funds for its support has not been particularly difficult and was aided by initially involving more than one faculty member in the work. Concern for how many students can reasonably be included in the actual work (and how those students would be selected to participate) dovetails with concerns about

NEW DIRECTIONS FOR HIGHER EDUCATION • DOI: 10.1002/he

department financial contributions. Whether the program can successfully transition beyond the lead faculty member is also a question, as is the consequence to relationships built should the department faculty opt to pursue this endeavor elsewhere at any given time rather than sustain this engagement only with this partner institution.

University Priority for Institutional Development. The final example emanates from a long-standing institutional commitment to working with an international university. Although heretofore the work was largely discipline-specific, five years ago faculty in our department were asked by central administration to conduct workshops focused on faculty development and organizational capacity building over a fifteen-day period one summer. Because return visits were requested, a total of four different department faculty participated during the first two years of involvement, and since then, one has stayed integrally involved, typically making two trips a year to conduct workshops, staff development, and assist with developing strategic plans for new faculty development initiatives. Throughout this period, there have been ongoing discussions of shared programs, recruiting master's and doctoral students, faculty exchanges, and the opportunity for student internships or research. Although a few international students have matriculated into the degree program, most of the rest of the discussions have borne no fruit for several reasons. The work has been intense, gratifying for the faculty champion, and remains essentially unfunded, although at times partially supported by department or university funds.

University-level arguments for sustained engagement have long been made for partnering with this particular international institution; yet, in more restricted financial times and with less clear in-country support from the institution or the ministry of education, priorities tend to shift at least somewhat, pushing the responsibility to support such partnerships down into the more local level of our university. A joint proposal was submitted to USAid last year to support the work but was not funded, though some ministry funding was obtained for some of the native institution's initiatives, but these monies did not come back to support our involvement. It is a key interest to the champion faculty member and some in our central administration to maintain involvement in this partnership, but the extent to which this remains a favorable site for outreach engagement is not clear. One could question the consequences of saying no to your university in terms of offering outreach support, as one could question what happens when your university changes its mind or priorities during your investment in an international project. At this point, the work is seen as only "Ted's thing" even while it draws down available department resources for local initiatives or other international partnerships in ways that are similar to and different from those experienced whenever any faculty member embarks on individual outreach or research activities. Assessing the overall cost-benefit of the initiative to our department is challenging.

NEW DIRECTIONS FOR HIGHER EDUCATION • DOI: 10.1002/he

Administrative Observations

International partnerships, including those referenced here, have some of the same benefits of domestic cross-institutional partnerships. These arrangements provide opportunities beyond those that individual institutions can do alone for faculty, students, research and outreach activity, and global understandings. They are often keys to innovation in resource-constrained environments and may connect to deeply held faculty and institutional priorities in improving practice at many levels. International partnerships also carry with them similar logistical issues to domestic collaborations, some of which are magnified in the implementation phase. For example, all institutions do not operate exactly the same way in regards to academic terms, faculty rewards, tuition models, and so on. Yet, acknowledging that there is a significant difference between how you support the time to build the trust and social capital to establish these initiatives cross-nationally (and cross-culturally) relative to creating domestic partnership is important.

Referring again to the partnership model (Amey, Eddy, and Ozaki, 2007), the first stage focuses on antecedents and the motivation for involvement and the context of the partnership, particularly as related to the champion who initiates it. In reviewing the cases outlined, the antecedents for establishing international partnerships were often, though not exclusively, quite local, resting with the interests, passions, and investment of individual faculty champions. It is clear that long-standing relationships were the genesis of our cross-national initiatives and the strength of these relationships can provide significant benefit at least to individuals and, often, there is capacity to benefit the larger unit, but how to expand the capital as a collective resource is not always clear. For example, the benefits of Fulbright Scholar Awards to individual faculty are well documented. The prestige and selectivity of the award brings recognition to the faculty member and is often used as a quality indicator in different program assessments. But, there is far less discussion of advantages accrued by departments that support faculty pursuing Fulbright grants (Amey, 2009). In times when resources are continually scrutinized and often shrinking, despite any benefits gained, department chairs have to carefully weigh the costs of covering an absent faculty member who receives a Fulbright or other form of sabbatical funding. As opposed to considering the Fulbright as only a benefit to the individual and a cost to the department, we need to see the possibilities potentially gained for departments when supporting those who participate in this prestigious international experience. And we need to act on those possibilities, which is a conscious reorientation towards the leave and a willingness to encourage partnership development on behalf of the collective by the recipient.

The second stage of the partnership model focuses on the partnership itself and how it develops beyond the initial motivations to participate (Amey, Eddy, and Ozaki, 2007). Each of the international partnerships referenced contributes to, or has contributed to the work of the department (and College and University) in different ways; notably, each is also of most benefit and cost to the champion faculty member. In our case, for different reasons, it is not apparent that any of our current international partnerships would be sustained without the champion because the projects are still primarily associated with that person and in three of four cases, only associated with that person. Broadening participation, understanding, and ownership of the partnership requires moving beyond the individual to the collective whole so that these would be considered organizational international partnerships rather than cross-border faculty dyads. Whether this transition happens or not is tied to understanding the experience beyond its original intent.

If the international partnership is to be owned by the department, several questions arise about the role of core faculty champions in the activity. What happens when a champion in either place (or a primary partner) retires, leaves the institution, or no longer wants to participate in the partnership? Do you close it down? Find another champion? Another partner? Has the partnership become institutionalized enough to live on beyond the original champion? If the relationship is built from an individual faculty member's social capital, to what extent should it be expanded to involve others? Given the distance and other associated costs involved, how does a department create the space for faculty to build the social capital from which international partnerships emerge, at least certain forms of these relationships?

Taking a step back from the activities themselves, in a way, each of these partnerships has gained a new, third partner: the department. Research on collaboration and partnerships, regardless of their location, notes that understanding mutual motivations for participation, benefits, and costs is important to establishing effective relationships and increasing the likelihood of sustaining them (Amey, Eddy, and Ozaki, 2007; Eddy, 2007; Farrell and Seifert, 2007; Gray, 1989; Sakamoto and Chapman, 2010). The interests and investment of this new partner are not antithetical to those of the faculty champions, nor are they always in tandem. As with other initiatives, administrators need to consider cost, logistical support, time on task and time away from campus, how faculty account for these activities in annual evaluation and promotion/tenure decisions, and the extent to which these ventures outweigh other experiences in which more students or faculty could easily be involved. Partnerships, international and domestic, are sometimes considered "fringe activities," risky, difficult to negotiate, political, and easily challenged by the institutional status quo (Amey and Brown, 2004; Fear, Creamer, Pirog, Block, and Redmond, 2004). For example, we do not typically give "credit" in terms of time or resources for developing a new class, and yet each of these experiences that involve instruction essentially was like constructing a new class, at least in terms of time on task. So how the time investment in relationship upkeep, logistical support, and so on, required for the partnership is accounted for is not clear or consistent.

NEW DIRECTIONS FOR HIGHER EDUCATION • DOI: 10.1002/he

Situating international partnerships as departmental, rather than individual activities, also changes aspects of the relationship that have to do with accountability and sustainability reflected in stage three of the partnership model (Amey, Eddy, and Ozaki, 2007). These factors may be defined differently from an administrative and collective perspective than if the partnership stayed only within the purview of a single faculty member. What is measured and how to signify impact and value (or productivity), how one moves individual passion into programmatic investment (and should you), and how the interests of others come into play all may get resolved within the structure of the department or academic unit, rather than at the individual faculty level; hence, the premise of a third partner in the relationship. When trying to build capacity for work such as international partnerships, administrators are often forced to consider the balance between new initiatives, more traditional core activities, and those that may be under greatest scrutiny by senior leaders, accrediting agencies, and program reviews. How we review new initiatives in other countries in our department involves decisions about competing interests and use of limited resources. With the four initiatives currently ongoing in our department, it is not clear how decisions regarding continued funding will occur, especially given needs of other domestic partnerships and new proposed international initiatives. If we add more, do we have to let go of these?

Even if we are trying to build capacity for international work and enhance our visibility and the international competencies of our students, how are the limits or parameters of such work determined? When resources are constrained and agendas compete, how should we think about international partnerships? How do we hold each other accountable for adding value if department resources are used to support the activity? Is the cost of engagement more than for domestic collaborations, or just assumed to be so because we may less carefully monitor the costs for work that has been traditionally part of the repertoire? How do we document the impact of these activities for students, faculty, and the culture of a unit? How do we hold the experiences in tandem with institutional guidelines for other faculty activities, for example, class size (for instance, it is hard to deliver international programming with our home students beyond the traditional tour model if enrollments have to be as high as is true for face-to-face); how does international course delivery fit in a funding model based on on-campus instruction? And as always with funded work, what happens when the original funding source dries up (a Fulbright, grant, sabbatical leave) if the resources to support become part of those allocated to other departmental activities? Are there differences between funded and unfunded collaborations? What is the impact of instructional versus research versus outreach forms of international partnership in how these issues are seen and ultimately negotiated? These issues are not germane only to international partnerships as they have been raised in research and practice historically when talking about outreach, service, online instruction, and other kinds of initiatives in which faculty participate (Fairweather, 2002).

NEW DIRECTIONS FOR HIGHER EDUCATION • DOI: 10.1002/he

Conclusion

International partnerships, like other cross-border collaborations, are often first understood as individual activities that benefit champion faculty and evoke costs from others not involved to support the work. And like their domestic counterparts, international partnerships are typically more complicated than at first appears; they may or may not achieve their stated objectives, and sustaining the partnership beyond the initial funding cycle is often challenging. If international engagement is an important component of the higher education landscape for the future, these activities need to become part of the core functions of departments and colleges rather than being relegated to the purview of individual faculty champions for their sustenance. This does not mean that they may not continue to be initiated by individuals based on particular research, outreach, or instructional passions, but like other aspects of the evolving academic enterprise, they cannot continue to be perceived as only the agenda of solo actors if the goal is infusion, greater impact on students and faculty, or enduring engagement. These goals require more institutionalization and collective commitment of resources, broadly defined, and greater ability to translate the activities into the accountability systems of the academy should they be program reviews, faculty evaluation criteria, or other institutional measures of productivity. As we all move forward with international partnerships, it will be important to continue studying their development and the ways in which they transition into the organizational culture so that we might establish effective strategies for supporting these activities and finding mutual benefit from them for all the partners involved.

References

Amey, M. J. "The Collective Benefits of Fulbright Exchanges." *Fulbright Center News,* 2009, *19*(2), 14–15.

Amey, M. J., and Brown, D. F. *Breaking Out of the Box: Interdisciplinary Collaboration and Faculty Work.* Boston: Information Age Publishing, 2004.

Amey, M. J., Eddy, P. L., and Campbell, T. G. "Crossing Boundaries: Creating Community College Partnerships to Promote Educational Transitions." *Community College Review,* 2010, *37*(4), 333–347.

Amey, M. J., Eddy, P. L., and Ozaki, C. C. "Demands for Partnership and Collaboration in Higher Education: A Model." In M. J. Amey (ed.), *Collaborations Across Educational Sectors.* New Directions for Community Colleges, no. 139. San Francisco: Jossey-Bass, 2007.

Black, T. H., and Duhon, D. L. "Assessing the Impact of Business Study Abroad Programs on Cultural Awareness and Personal Development." *Journal of Education for Business,* 2006, *81*(3), 140–144.

Eddy, P. L. "Alliances Among Community Colleges: Odd Bedfellows or Lasting Partners?" In M. J. Amey (ed.), *Collaborations Across Educational Sectors.* New Directions for Community Colleges, no. 139. San Francisco: Jossey-Bass, 2007.

Fairhurst, G. T., and Sarr, R. A. *The Art of Framing: Managing the Language of Leadership.* San Francisco: Jossey-Bass, 1996.

Fairweather, J. S. "The Ultimate Faculty Evaluation: Promotion and Tenure Decisions." In C. L. Colbeck (ed.), *Evaluating Faculty Performance*. New Directions for Teaching and Learning, no. 114. San Francisco: Jossey-Bass, 2002.

Farrell, P. L., and Seifert, K. A. "Lessons Learned From a Dual-enrollment Partnership." In M. J. Amey (ed.), *Collaborations Across Educational Sectors*. New Directions for Community Colleges, no. 139. San Francisco: Jossey-Bass, 2007.

Fear, F., Creamer, N., Pirog, R., Block, D., and Redmond, L. "Higher Education–Community Partnerships: The Politics of Engagement." *Journal of Higher Education Outreach and Engagement*, 2004, 9(2), 139–156.

Gray, B. *Collaborating: Finding Common Ground for Multiparty Problems*. San Francisco: Jossey-Bass, 1989.

Kitsantas, A. "Studying Abroad: The Role of College Students' Goals on the Development of Cross-Cultural Skills and Global Understanding." *College Student Journal*, 2004, 38(3), 441–452

Lindsey, E. W. "Study Abroad and Values Development in Social Work Students." *Journal of Social Work Education*, 2005, 41(2), 229–249.

Morgan, G. *Images of Organization* (2nd ed.). Thousand Oaks, Calif.: Sage, 1998.

Ozaki, C. C., Amey, M. J., and Watson, J. S. "Strategies for the Future." In M. J. Amey (ed.), *Collaborations Across Educational Sectors*. New Directions for Community Colleges, no. 139. San Francisco: Jossey-Bass, 2007.

Sakamoto, R., and Chapman, D. W. *Cross-Border Collaborations in Higher Education: Partnerships Beyond the Classroom*. New York: Routledge, 2010.

Tornatzky, L. G., and Fleischer, M. *The Processes of Technological Innovation*. Lexington, Mass.: Lexington Books, 1990.

Weick, K. E. *Sensemaking in Organizations*. Thousand Oaks, Calif.: Sage, 1995.

Wolverton, M. "Champions, Agents, and Collaborators: Leadership Keys to Successful Systemic Change." *Journal of Higher Education Policy and Management*, 1998, 20(1), 19–30.

Young, D. Y. "Participation in a Study-Abroad Program and Persistence at a Liberal Arts University." Unpublished doctoral dissertation Thesis, University of North Texas, 2003.

MARILYN J. AMEY *is professor and chair of the Department of Higher, Adult, and Lifelong Education at Michigan State University.*

NEW DIRECTIONS FOR HIGHER EDUCATION • DOI: 10.1002/he

6

This chapter examines the incentives and challenges faculty are facing as they become involved in international collaborations at the program, course, and individual level.

Faculty Perspectives on International Education: The Nested Realities of Faculty Collaborations

Joanne Cooper, Rikki Mitsunaga

As institutions of higher education strive to project the "image of a well-connected university," they frequently develop strategic international networks or alliances with colleges and universities around the globe (Higgitt and others, 2008, p. 121). According to Altbach and Knight (2007), the main motivation to internationalize is not for financial gain, but to "enhance research and knowledge capacity and to increase cultural understanding" (p. 291) as well as "enhance competitiveness, prestige and strategic alliances" (p. 293) for the university.

Faculty clearly plays a key role in any university's international efforts. Bottery (2006) argues that faculty members need to be more aware of the global factors that affect their professional practice, because "without such awareness, professionals are blind to the changes affecting their societies and their own practice" (p. 106). Stohl (2007) states that universities must work to engage faculty interest in international activities by underscoring the rewards in learning and discovery that are possible. These rewards include learning about, learning from, and learning with others, all of which enrich the lives of faculty with better scholarship and "the recognition by their colleagues and institutions that this is a worthwhile activity that should be rewarded" (Stohl, 2007, p. 369).

Even though faculty are obviously vital to the work of internationalizing academia, "surprisingly little work has been published that addresses the roles, responsibilities, and problems faced by faculty on an operational

NEW DIRECTIONS FOR HIGHER EDUCATION, no. 150, Summer 2010 © Wiley Periodicals, Inc.
Published online in Wiley InterScience (www.interscience.wiley.com) • DOI: 10.1002/he.391

level" (Dewey and Duff, 2009, p. 491). The experiences of faculty who participate in cross-institutional, cross-national collaborations, the motivations behind their willingness to engage in this work, and the forces that support or hinder their work are relatively unknown. In fact, current global forces at work on universities and the challenges of cross-cultural collaborations that they bring are often added to the traditional requirements for faculty to juggle the roles of teaching, research, and service. Three things happen when today's faculty members enter the challenging arena of international collaborations:

- Faculty members leave the safety of their traditional classrooms and enter a broader and more complex world of global interactions that are often market driven.
- They encounter cross-cultural challenges that are often unanticipated and for which they may be ill-equipped.
- They encounter collaborative challenges, which can be accompanied by technological challenges.

This chapter examines the motivations, supports, and barriers faculty are facing as they become involved in international collaborations. We have described these experiences as "nested realities" simply because faculty may find themselves involved in collaborations at the individual level, at the classroom level, and at the program level as they work to deliver educational opportunities for students in all these ways.

Collaboration and Motivation

Scholars involved in international collaborative efforts have identified key issues for institutional consideration: how to build and sustain relationships, how to make things happen (catalytic events), and the role of common and divergent understandings (Shore and Groen, 2009). Central elements include shared professional interests, personal affinities, and institutional agreements or structures that smooth the way for collaborative efforts (Amey and Brown, 2004). Although countries and cultures may vary in their values and viewpoints, an examination of the best educational systems in the world highlight the recruitment of good people, the employment of continuous staff development, the expectation of success, and good leadership (Crow, 2009). Others warn against an imbalance in the relationship that may endanger the goals of mutual respect required in collaborations (Psaltis, 2007), and reciprocity in the co-construction of knowledge (Amey, Eddy, and Ozaki, 2007).

Key to faculty roles in partnerships is individual and organizational motivations. Motivation theories generally fall into two categories: extrinsic and intrinsic. Extrinsic motivation theorists (economists) assert that people are rational and always strive to maximize rewards, often financial in form (Blackburn and Lawrence, 1995). For faculty this may take the form of promotions, public recognition of good works, or extra resources. Intrinsic motivation theorists (psychologists) assert that behavior follows internal desires and interests and believe that faculty, when they are free to choose, will continue to do what interests them, despite external rewards. Both extrinsic and intrinsic motivators are often at work in the lives of faculty. Perhaps Blackburn and Lawrence (1995) best summarized faculty motivation in their statement that faculty often "do what they believe they are good at (self-competence), devote energy to what interests them. . .[and] engage in activities in which they can influence the outcomes (efficiency)" (p. 281).

Methods and Cases Studies

This study utilized three qualitative case studies of faculty from two universities, one in the United States and one in New Zealand. Participants were identified through purposeful sampling (Merriam, 2009). The faculty represents a wide variety of collaborative possibilities: a faculty member (and former associate dean) who serves others in small Pacific Island nations, an ethnomusicologist who teaches online courses across national borders, and a business professor who runs a twenty-year-old joint U.S./ Japan Masters of Business Administration program. The cases represent collaborative efforts on the individual, course, and program level. Data were gathered through individual interviews and documents review, including course outlines and program descriptions. Individual cases were developed and analyzed in two stages, within-case analysis and then cross-case analysis (Merriam, 2009). Each case was presented to participants for member-checking.

While faculty may be working at all three levels of engagement—the individual, classroom, and program level—in keeping with our theme of nested realities, the cases are presented in order of increasing size. First, the case of Dr. Jane Strachan at the University of Waikato describes her work on the island of Vanuatu and as the director of the Solomon Islands School of Education Partnership (SISEP). Second, we present the case of Dr. Ricardo Trimillos, from the University of Hawaii, who has been involved for the last nine years in an online chat course that serves students in both Hawaii and the Philippines. Finally, we present the case of Dr. Stan Findling, faculty director of a joint Japan/U.S. Masters of Business Administration (MBA) for the past eight years.

Case Study I: Doing Heart Work. Jane Strachan has been a faculty member at the University of Waikato in New Zealand for eighteen years. During that time she has developed an international reputation as a feminist scholar. She serves in the School of Education and has been involved in two cross-cultural partnerships, the first on the individual level and the second at the program level.

Eight years ago Jane was "caught up in administration" when the opportunity to work in Vanuatu, a part of Melanesia in the Pacific, through the Volunteer Services Abroad (VSA) program, became available. This work seemed "more exciting, more challenging and more interesting" to her and provided an opportunity for her to "walk the talk of my feminist and social justice" research agenda. "It just grabbed my heart," she says. This experience involved a lot of "learning on the job." Jane stated, "I didn't know how to work in the culture." Vanuatu is a complex culture with one hundred ten indigenous languages. The first thing she did was learn Bislama, a form of English/French pidgin that is the lingua franca of the country. She said, "It took me six months to become functional," and to be able to give workshops and write documents in the language. Jane took a two-year leave without pay from her job and then a six-month study leave, serving as Women's Advisor to the Director of the Department of Women's Affairs. When her leave was up, Jane had to return to the university, but her work in Vanuatu continues today, chiefly in the form of small research projects.

Jane's second cross-cultural collaboration began almost four years ago when she became involved in a new partnership, the Solomon Island School of Education Partnership, a collaboration between the School of Education at the University of Waikato and the Solomon Islands College of Higher Education. She had "fallen in love with Melanesia" and "grieved for the work" she had left in Vanuatu. Because of her familiarity with the local culture in Vanuatu, Jane was asked to help write a proposal to work in the war-torn Solomon Islands. Through a multi-million-dollar grant from the New Zealand government (NZAID) she now leads a project to build teacher education in the Solomon Islands. The project involved finding faculty in her college who were willing to travel and work there, designing five new teacher qualifications and eighty new courses in what she calls lots of "seat of the pants" work. They went in "not as consultants" but as partners, an important distinction for a place that had been "developed to death" with many expensive consultants coming in for brief stays, leaving behind resentment and little ownership of change.

Jane noted that both projects have been "blessed with a very supportive administration." The work is emotionally and physically exhausting. Travel to both projects took several days and involved "eating, planning, working, and debriefing" together from early in the morning until late at night. The camaraderie that the faculty built in the Solomons provides a support for the work. Jane counts her family as another support. They have taken an interest in her work and are proud of what she's done. She smiles and says, "They like telling their friends about it."

Although NZAID, which funded the Solomon Island project, has been supportive, "it has not always been an easy relationship" partly because of the strong accountability agenda. One of the greatest challenges to both projects has been "being viewed as a white expert." Jane worked hard to develop relationships in both locations. She says, "Melanesians are extremely polite" so it is sometimes hard to know if they really agree with you and "nothing happens if they don't." Building relationships meant trying to overcome the long history of colonization in the Pacific. For example, if you are walking along the street and two people meet in the narrow track, "the local people step off." "Instead," Jane says, "I try to beat them to it and step off first."

Another big challenge is the differing concept of time. "We're driven by time" but in Melanesia, "things happen in a circular way." Forward planning is not a part of the culture. "They are people of the moment," so trying to do strategic long-range planning can be extremely difficult. Also, because these are small island cultures, relationships are extremely important, so if you are on your way to a meeting and you meet your cousins, it is more important to chat with them than to make it to the meeting on time. After years in both locations Jane says that trusting relationships are finally building. "They are beginning to tell me their secrets" and to share more of their personal lives with her.

Jane reflected that relationship building is "everything" in this work. "Nothing will happen without this." It is especially important when a developed country is working with a "least developed" country, especially one with a history of colonization. Although learning the language is not mandatory, it does help and her knowledge of Bislama has been useful.

Both partnerships involved personal investment by faculty. Jane took a leave without pay to work in Vanuatu and faculty in the Solomon Islands project work there as part of their normal teaching load, not as paid consultants. Jane stresses that both parties have to want the partnership to happen and that both sides must see benefits to the work. One of the benefits for New Zealand, for example, is that this work helps them to fulfill their obligation to their Pacific neighbors. Another unanticipated benefit has been the flood of students who have come from the Solomons to study at the university. Unfortunately, although this has benefited the university, it has been a drain on the expertise in the Solomon Islands. These students will go back after they finish their studies, but in the meantime, the country suffers from this loss.

Because this work is both time and energy consuming, Jane stresses that you must take care of yourself. In addition, it is important to take care of the relationship between the partners. "Keep in regular communication. Don't let too much time lapse." This can be difficult because the Internet can be down for days at a time, but it is really important to stay in touch. There is little doubt that thus far these collaborations have been extremely successful and have benefited both partners, sometimes in ways they little imagined at the beginning of their mutual journeys.

Case Study II: Running an International Online Chat Course. Ric Trimillos is an award-winning ethnomusicologist from the Asian Studies Department at the University of Hawaii, recently receiving the Distinguished Graduate Mentoring Award from the University. Today, in search of his exquisite teacher-self, we climb the four floors to his office and are greeted by a child's drawing of red flowers and a sun on his door addressed to "Uncle Ric" with a note below that states, "At least I have one fan. . . ." But Ric has many fans, both in the United States and across the Pacific. His international collaborative efforts include work with universities in Japan and the Philippines in the areas of Kabuki Theater, music, and Asian Studies.

One of his most successful and long-running projects has been an online chat course between Hawaii and the Philippines entitled "Researching Area Studies: Sovereignty, Settlers and Land Use." This effort started with a Ford Foundation Grant in 2000 and focused on collaborative pedagogy and peer learning, "not just scholars talking to each other." The grant allowed both faculty and students to travel back and forth between Hawaii and the Philippines. At the end of the grant, a conference was held that involved faculty and students from both universities. There were five original projects in Fiji, Singapore, Japan, and New Zealand (as well as this one in the Philippines), all run by different faculty members on campus. But Ric's program is the only one to continue after the funding ran out. He noted, "Both sides wanted to keep it going." The project involves a partnership with the Jesuit University Ateneo De Zamboaga (ADZU) in the Southern Philippines. It is a partial online class: On Tuesdays the classes meet face to face and on Thursdays they meet online. The online chat portion of the class runs on Thursdays from 4:30 to 5:45 p.m. in Hawaii, which is Friday from 10:30 to 11:45 a.m. in the Philippines. The Hawaii students like this arrangement because they don't have to come to class on Thursdays because they can be online anywhere.

One of the key elements in the course is its emphasis on peer learning and on "seeing the relevance of lived experience." For example, the students in Hawaii feel free to argue among themselves about what it means to be "local," whereas the Filipino students freely discuss Muslim/Christian issues in their country. Ric says the students are able to ask "dumb" questions of each other that come out of their naïve honesty, which pushes critical thinking in each setting. If a student makes a statement that is way off, inevitably another student will step in and correct it. Ric says that the faculty members who are involved in the course have to be alert to the "teachable moments" in the discussion and dive in with helpful information at the right time.

The similar histories of colonialism and land-use issues in both countries in addition to the numbers of Filipinos in Hawaii have helped to cement this course-level partnership. Ric's department is steeped in interdisciplinary work and supports the course. The department honors collaborative work and alternative ways of learning and has provided material support in the form of travel funds for its faculty. The grant provided initial funding for computer equipment in the Philippines and the previous and current university presidents continue to support the project, despite some rumblings about the project "hogging" computers on their campus. Even with the change in presidents, ADZU has continued to support this project because the university has seen marginal students get excited about learning through this course. Many of their students have grown more self-confident, stepping into important leadership roles as a result of this course. Some have joined nongovernmental organizations (NGOs) in the Philippines; American students have gone on to work with minority groups in California or social action projects in Hawaii. For many students this course has been "a life changing experience."

Ric states that "it's the chemistry of what goes on" that makes the collaboration work. The egalitarian attitudes of the project participants have helped to support the work and over time the Filipino participants have become "more proactive" in contributing ideas for the project, such as topics of discussion. Language commonalities have also helped the collaboration. "One guy is Tausūg . . . which means I can talk to him in the language of his comfort rather than always in English," states Ric. The other American professor speaks fluent Ilocano, which delights the Filipino participants when he visits.

The differing academic calendars present a major challenge. The academic term in the Philippines begins in June and ends in October. Hawaii's semester begins in August and ends in December. This splits the class into three phases, the first with more Filipino students in the classroom, the second with a full complement of students at both sites, and the third with more U.S. students in attendance. Ric says the project would not succeed without "a strong commitment to start early and go late" by both faculty and even some students.

To start a successful academic collaboration, Ric believes that it is important to "find cooperative counterparts on the other side." In their case, it was partly "serendipitous," in that the President of ADZU was coming through Hawaii on his way to a conference in Washington D.C. and met one of the grant participants in a meeting at the East/West Center. As president of a private university, he had the power to make decisions, provide release time for his faculty there and help get the project off the ground. Three years ago a new president was hired who cancelled the release time for faculty, but the rewards of being able to travel to Hawaii as a visiting scholar have encouraged their faculty to continue with the course.

Ric believes that collaborators must "be open to other pedagogical goals and strategies." If the attitude is "it's my course," the collaboration has less chance of success. He notes you also must remember that "students are not dumb. In order to teach, we don't have to control." He believes that faculty must act "not as gatekeepers, but as referees." It is clear from our discussion that he has tremendous faith in the ability of students to think critically and deeply about the topics presented in class and to handle thoughtful cross-cultural conversations with skill and ability. Finally, Ric reflected you must make sure that both sides of the collaboration have the technical equipment needed for the project. The Ford Foundation grant was very helpful in

NEW DIRECTIONS FOR HIGHER EDUCATION • DOI: 10.1002/he

obtaining the initial equipment and the university was committed to keeping it upgraded.

It is not surprising that Ric Trimillos has just won an award for his work in mentoring students. His respect for students' ability and his delight in their learning radiated throughout our discussion. "Uncle Ric" has more than one fan and he is richly deserving of them all, given his skillful dedication to students both at home and across the globe.

Case Study III: International Collaborative Program Efforts. In many ways, Stan Findling's office is typical of a university professor's. Books and papers are stacked about. Yet despite its haphazard appearance, there is a suggestion of purposefulness and design. Stan has won numerous service and teaching awards, and is widely published with an extensive and impressive dossier. He teaches both graduate and undergraduate business courses. His welcoming smile belies the serious nature of the tasks he wrestles with as the Faculty Director for the Japan-focused Masters of Business Administration (Japan MBA) program and his responses to our questions were at times both warm and surprisingly blunt.

According to Stan, who has been faculty director for eight years, his role is to "facilitate the smooth operation of the program but also to make sure there is institutional support for the program." He underscores that programs and initiatives require a champion and "faculty directors have traditionally been the champions of the programs they're involved in."

The Japan MBA program was established as a joint venture between the University's Business School and the Japan Management Institute (JMI). The program introduces MBA students to Japanese culture, develops their Japanese language skills, provides a daytime MBA curriculum, and culminates with a three-month corporate internship in Japan. Stan proudly emphasizes that "the internship was one of the distinguishing features of the program." JMI is responsible for providing the language and culture courses, and coordinates the internship opportunities for the students; and the college provides the MBA curriculum along with the faculty and administrative support.

In the formative years, he explained, JMI would annually award 15 scholarships provided by a private Japanese business firm and used those scholarships as "kind of a good will tool" to recruit students from all over Asia. The funding was the "economic driver" of the Japan MBA program. The intent was to provide Japan MBA students with an educational experience infused with cultural competence through firsthand living and working in Japan. In 2006, the school made programmatic and curriculum changes to the daytime MBA format, impacting the Japan MBA and the relationship with JMI.

When asked about the challenges he encountered, Stan clarified that the challenges he faced prior to 2006 were different from the challenges he faces today. Prior to 2006, the most significant and foremost challenge was "the economic viability of the . . . program. It was . . . on its own . . . it had to be financially justified. And that was really the challenge—to get the number of students to the point where we could achieve that." He shared that the program enrolled approximately twenty-five students annually, but needed thirty-five to forty students to be economically viable and "there were a few times when we got that, but it was very difficult to sustain. That was one of the reasons why the changes were made in 2006."

Stan pointed to the then twelve-month accelerated program as a second challenge. Prior to 2006, Japan MBA students were enrolled in forty-five credits of MBA courses plus Japanese language and culture lessons during the first twelve months. Then they participated in a three-month internship to finish the fifteen-month program. He reasons "at that speed, I always felt that it was pedagogically inappropriate so I had always lobbied for extending the length of the program." In 2006, the program was extended in length and that provided economic viability with the new MBA format allowing for a common first-year core, diverging in the second year to country-specific areas (i.e., Japan, China). The result extended the Japan MBA program to a twenty-month format (including the three-month internship) and removed the initial pressure of the Japan MBA's economic viability. Although the 2006 changes eliminated some program challenges, it added new challenges for Stan.

Among his challenges as faculty director, Stan notes, "My most significant problems have been where administrators are making decisions that I don't agree with. Decisions that I think are not in the interest of the students and not in the interest . . . [of] the quality of the program . . . driven in part by a lack of understanding about what the program is and what the program means to students." Stan believes some decisions are made because of a "preoccupation with program rankings."

He recounts a particular situation in which he recommended allowing the Japan MBA students the flexibility to make their own decision (e.g., take time off, participate in a local or international internship, or take a class) during the second summer session. Stan explained that "somebody on the administrative side said we shouldn't allow our students to be free . . . [in] the second summer term, so we're going to require them to take *a course . . .* and the course they're going to take is Japanese Management." Stan explained that "two undesirable things happened" as a result of "seemingly unilateral decisions." First, he lost the faculty member from Japan who could only teach the Japanese Management course in the fall semester and the replacement faculty did not work out. Second, students were frustrated at having to take only one course which required them to be on the campus.

The 2006 program changes resulted in a shift of administrative responsibilities from the Executive Education Office to the Office of Student Academic Services. Stan recounts that as a result routine administrative tasks that range from hiring and paying faculty, getting courses listed, and photocopying have "just been a freaking nightmare." These tasks, which were carried out by less than enthusiastic department staff, are now slowly being assigned as responsibilities are clarified and delegated.

When asked about the rewards of this work, Stan responded, "the most rewarding aspects for me, for any program I'm involved with, is seeing the students succeed. I think . . . that's what makes everything worthwhile. Seeing the students succeed and seeing the program maintain its momentum . . . continue to be viable."

Stan wishes he had more Japanese background, surmising that it would be beneficial if the faculty director of the Japan MBA program had "more Japanese experience, could speak Japanese, had lived in Japan, that sort of thing." Yet, what he lacks in country-specific expertise, he makes up in other ways. During his tenure as faculty director, Stan has maintained a good working relationship with JMI and the Japan MBA students. He speculates,

> I think that the most important success factor of a faculty director is . . . caring . . . not only caring but acting like you care . . . making sure I stay in touch with . . . JMI. Listening to them. Communicating with them. Staying in touch with the students . . . making sure you follow up with what their concerns are, let them know the updates . . . do the best you can in those regards.

Stan brings the Japan MBA students together once or twice a semester. They eat pizza, sit around, and talk. This deeper connectedness with his students is what makes him popular—the face-to-face time, and wanting to delve beyond the surface of "what's going on" to a richer conversation, which according to him, is finding out "what works, what doesn't." Stan Findling is an educator who clearly sees the value of preparing future business leaders for the global arena and as the Japan MBA faculty director, he has been a true champion.

Conclusions and Implications

These three cases illustrate faculty involvement in international collaborative efforts at the individual, classroom, and program level. Although one might describe these levels as nested, they are not fixed, but rather fluid and interconnected. Jane's initial involvement was at the individual level when she worked in Vanuatu as a VSA volunteer. Later she moved to the programmatic level, running a multi-million-dollar teacher education program in the Solomon Islands. Ric works at the classroom level, but has just won an award for mentoring individual students, and Stan, who has run an international MBA program for eight years, stresses the importance of caring for students on an individual level.

A key factor across the cases is that all faculty participants have been successful in their partnerships. Thus, it is interesting to note what motivates them to continue this work, as well as what advice they would give others. Much of their motivation seems to be intrinsic. Jane describes it as "heart work." Stan states that it is caring for students that keeps him involved and Ric talks about the satisfaction of watching students learn and grow. Extrinsic rewards, such as funding and travel, seem to have more importance in the initial stages of these international efforts, when there is a need for equipment or when faculty are being recruited for a particular project. Notably, even when external funding was discontinued, the partnerships continued. Ric's Ford Foundation grant ran out and Stan's program became less self-sustaining over time. Both of these faculty members then sought support from their home institutions. Ric relies on travel funding from his department, whereas Stan's program was assimilated into the existing masters program in his college. This outcome is consistent with the work of Amey, Eddy, and Ozaki (2007) who assert that for the health of a partnership, it must eventually become part of the culture and administrative processes of an organization.

The question is what motivated these faculty members to seek continuation of their projects after they ran into fiscal trouble. Here the intrinsic rewards of the work seem to play a part. These faculty members state that they have continued their efforts due to intrinsic rewards, predominately in their deep satisfaction in working with students. At this point, few universities include international collaborative work in their external reward structures, beyond asking if the faculty member has an international reputation in research (Stohl, 2007). Granted, all our participants were tenured and thus not so tied to the university's reward structure. Our research supports Stohl's argument that colleges and universities must emphasize the intrinsic benefits of international work to engage faculty, to underscore the opportunities and benefits of learning and discovery that come with cross-cultural collaborative efforts.

Our findings also support the assertions by Psaltis (2007) and Amey, Eddy, and Ozaki (2007) that mutual respect and reciprocity between the collaborative partners is extremely important. The faculty in our cases continually struggle to form and maintain equitable relationships that benefit both parties in these cross-cultural, cross-national collaborations. Jane talks about trying to "beat the Solomon Islanders" in stepping off the footpath when they meet, as well as her efforts to establish professional collegial relationships in the collaboration. Ric also stresses his efforts to form egalitarian relationships with his Filipino partners. Both Jane and Ric used their language skills to smooth these partnerships and create connections that last. Stan laments his inability to speak Japanese and searches for ways to compensate for his lack of cross-cultural skills. All three understand the importance of relationship building, although Jane put it most succinctly when she warned, "Nothing will happen without this."

One key element in maintaining healthy relationships with collaborative partners is the effort to stay in touch. Both Jane and Stan mentioned the importance of regular communications with partners and it is clear that they work hard to keep the lines of communication open. Stan talked about listening to both collaborative partners and students. While Amey, Eddy, and

Ozaki (2007) discuss the importance of feedback, they do not specifically mention listening. Feedback has little impact if partners are not listening. We also see listening carefully, which may include embracing multiple and differing viewpoints, as a vital part of any cross-cultural interaction. Thus, staying in touch and listening are both key to faculty collaborative efforts.

According to scholars, a second set of relationships are also important to successful collaborations, those between faculty and their funding agencies or administrative bodies (Amey, Eddy, and Ozaki, 2007; Psaltis, 2007). This seems to be a more complex issue for our participants. As Jane stated, the university's relationship to their funding agency "has not always been easy." Stan, too, expressed his frustration with the administrative structures in his college and the movement of his program to a new administrative home. Although this change helped to give the program more security, it brought him into contact with a new set of support personnel, an experience he describes as "a freaking nightmare." It is clear that these relationships are complex, simultaneously providing support and barriers to the collaborative work.

Finally, staying flexible is central to the success of these international endeavors. Ric stressed that faculty must be open to other pedagogical goals and strategies. Rigid control of events with an attitude that "it's my course" is a barrier to successful collaborations. As Ric stated, "In order to teach, we don't have to control." Stan mentions this in the context of rigid administrative course requirements that frustrated both him and his students. The belief that students are not dumb and the flexibility to allow them some autonomy come through in their comments. This flexibility is also an important element of working across cultures with collaborative partners.

As institutions of higher education become more involved in international collaborative efforts, due to their desire to appear well-connected, to enhance their prestige and increase strategic alliances, as well as to compete in an increasingly global context (Altbach and Knight, 2007; Higgitt and others, 2008), faculty who are able to build and sustain long-term collaborations will play a key role. The lessons learned from successful faculty such as those in this study will be invaluable. Colleges and universities need to understand what entices faculty to begin cross-national collaborations and what sustains their work over time. In addition, the barriers to success will need to be clearly anticipated and understood in the hope that faculty and their institutions can avoid the pitfalls of their predecessors.

References

Altbach, P. G., and Knight, J. "The Internationalization of Higher Education: Motivations and Realities." *Journal of Studies in International Education*, 2007, *11*(3/4), 290–305.

Amey, M. J., and Brown, D. F. *Breaking Out of the Box: Interdisciplinary Collaboration and Faculty Work*. Boston: Information Age Publishing, 2004.

Amey, M. J., Eddy, P. L., and Ozaki, C. C. "Demands for Partnership and Collaboration in Higher Education: A Model." In M. J. Amey (ed.), *Collaborations Across Educational Sectors*. New Directions for Community Colleges, no. 139. San Francisco: Jossey-Bass, 2007, 5–16.

Blackburn, J., and Lawrence, J. *Faculty at Work: Motivation, Expectation, Satisfaction.* Baltimore: Johns Hopkins University Press, 1995.

Bottery, M. "Education and Globalization: Redefining the Role of the Educational Professional." *Educational Review,* 2006, *58*(1), 95–113.

Crow, T. "What Works, Works Everywhere." *Journal of Staff Development,* 2009, *30*(1), 10–16.

Dewey, P., and Duff, S. "Reason Before Passion: Faculty Views on Internationalization in Higher Education." *Higher Education,* 2009, *58,* 491–504.

Higgitt, D., Donert, K., Healey, M., Klein, P., Solem, M., and Vajoczki, S. "Developing and Enhancing International Collaborative Learning." *Journal of Geography in Higher Education,* 2008, *32*(1), 121–133.

Merriam, S. *Qualitative Research: A Guide to Design and Implementation.* San Francisco: Jossey-Bass, 2009.

Psaltis, C. "International Collaboration as Construction of Knowledge and Its Constraints." *Integrative Psychological and Behavioral Science,* 2007, *41,* 187–197.

Shore, S., and Groen, J. "After the Ink Dries: Doing Collaborative International Work in Higher Education." *Studies in Higher Education,* 2009, *34*(5), 533–546.

Stohl, M. "We Have Met the Enemy and He Is Us: The Role of the Faculty in the Internationalization of Higher Education in the Coming Decade." *Journal of Studies in International Education,* 2007, *11*(3/4), 359–372.

JOANNE COOPER *is professor of Educational Administration at the University of Hawaii, Manoa.*

RIKKI MITSUNAGA *is a doctoral student at the College of Education at the University of Hawaii, Manoa, and an undergraduate academic advisor at the University of Hawaii, Manoa.*

7

Liberal arts colleges face particular challenges in using insti-
tutional partnerships as a vehicle for internationalization.

Leveraging Partnerships to Internationalize the Liberal Arts College: Campus Internationalization and the Faculty

Elizabeth Brewer

Small, liberal arts colleges can be unlikely partners for international partnerships. With limited numbers of faculty members, a focus on teaching rather than research, educational facilities as opposed to research facilities, and undergraduate populations, they often are looked at skeptically by potential partners in countries with no liberal arts tradition and where value is associated with research rankings rather than quality of instruction. Nevertheless, international partnerships with liberal arts colleges can serve both receiving and sending institutions. Further, for liberal arts institutions in particular, partnerships with universities in other countries can offer opportunities to help them internationalize the campus. Although the exchange of students may remain the basis for most institutional partnerships, a focus on using the partnerships to internationalize the faculty, and through them the curriculum, can have lasting, positive effects on the teaching and learning taking place on the liberal arts campus. Activities beyond the exchange of students, however, require that partnerships be grounded in institutional strategies and have faculty ownership.

This chapter provides a review of study abroad and partnerships within the context of liberal arts colleges. Particular attention is given to the role of faculty and the internationalization of the curriculum. A case study of a partnership between Beloit College in Wisconsin and Henan University, a

New Directions for Higher Education, no. 150, Summer 2010 © Wiley Periodicals, Inc.
Published online in Wiley InterScience (www.interscience.wiley.com) • DOI: 10.1002/he.392

Chinese university located in Kaifeng, Henan Province, provides an example of how internationalization can be coupled with opportunities for faculty development to maximize the benefits of an institutional partnership.

The Liberal Arts College: Alignment with Internationalization

Higher education in the United States has been associated with liberal education from its very beginnings. As opposed to education for specific trades and professions, the intent of liberal education is, as Nussbaum (2007) argues, to cultivate "the whole human being for the functions of citizenship and life in general" (p. 37). This view echoes an early report by the Yale College Corporation (Committee, 1828) that underscored the purpose of a broad education. Beloit College, founded by graduates of New England colleges and chartered in 1846 in the Territory of Wisconsin, was to follow in the Yale College tradition of teaching students "how to learn" (Nussbaum, 2007, p. 14).

The Association of American Colleges and Universities (AAC&U) characterizes liberal education in the twentieth century as an "an option for the fortunate," "non-vocational," and "involving intellectual and personal development" (AAC&U, 2009a, ¶5). However, it argues that in the twenty-first century, liberal education must be extended to all students because it is "essential for success in a global economy and for informed citizenship" (AAC&U, 2009b, ¶1). Supporting this, the 2005 Lincoln Commission report that gave rise to the 2007 Senator Paul Simon Study Abroad Foundation Act (H.R. 1469 and S. 991), stated that participation in study abroad, one of the components of international education, must increase dramatically if Americans are to be able to participate fully in the global workforce.

Liberal education is, of course, at the core of the liberal arts college. The liberal arts college is largely a U.S. phenomenon, with a focus on undergraduate teaching. Although a number of countries have established versions of liberal arts institutions to promote such skills as critical thinking, the small, residential, undergraduate, liberal arts institution is relatively rare even within the United States. Thus, although many liberal arts institutions claim an international character, their small size, focus on undergraduate teaching, and lack of large research agendas and facilities separate them from many institutions of higher education in other countries. Further, as Tillman (2007) notes in NAFSA's Guide to Interuniversity Linkages, many universities seeking partners in the United States hope for agreements with "prestigious colleges and universities" (p. xii). As evidenced in Germany's recent "excellence initiative" to identify top-level institutions for further support, prestige is most often associated only with "research [with] the importance of excellence in teaching . . . relegated as a second-rate qualification" (Kehm, 2009, p. 19). Similarly, Chinese universities tend to look for partners that will "improve . . . institutional reputation, and increase their competitive advantage on the world stage and in the international market-place of ideas" (Julius, 2009, ¶14) and thus the potential partner's national and international ranking will play an important role. The desire for prestige makes the liberal arts college, which enters into rankings on a very different basis, an unnatural partner for many universities elsewhere in the world, including China. As discussed later in this chapter, however, a partnership between institutions with different aims and characteristics can work, if the institutions understand the scope of such a partnership and can find opportunities for mutual benefit.

Study Abroad in the Liberal Arts Context

Founded in 1846 with its first classes taking place the following year, Beloit College's first steps toward internationalization were associated with the same kind of drive that led to the college's creation: a belief that one of the duties of educated men was to spread opportunities for higher education. Beloit College's alumni were traveling abroad as early as 1851 as teaching missionaries. Returning to campus to lecture about their experiences and the lands visited, they also sent reports, photos, and other documentation of their travels, thereby connecting the college to the larger world (Siegel, 1992). International students were enrolling in the college by 1853.

The internationalization of U.S. education has long been associated with study abroad, although today most scholars of international education see study abroad as merely one component of an internationalization strategy (American Council on Education, 1995). Nevertheless, it is important for the purposes of this chapter to reflect on the significance of study abroad within liberal education. Modern study abroad in the United States came into being in 1923, when Delaware College, now the University of Delaware, sent a group of eight students to France for their junior year. Other American colleges and universities previously had seen students, faculty, and alumni go abroad to acquire international experience and broaden their cultural and linguistic horizons. The Delaware College initiative, however, marked the beginning of undergraduate sojourns abroad as an activity earning credit toward the degree at the home institution. This definition of study abroad as a credit-bearing activity remains operational in the United States today (Hoffa, 2007). Further, as argued by Gore (2005), study abroad from the start was meant to be academically rigorous and an activity that would contribute to the preparation of students for professional life and citizenship. As such, it resonated closely with the goals of liberal education.

Further, study abroad also has long been associated with the liberal arts college because the educational goals of study abroad and liberal arts institutions mesh. Institutional commitment, however, has been equally important, and thus many liberal arts colleges have made study abroad possible for their students by providing a variety of opportunities and permitting financial aid to support them. Notably, institutions with the highest study

NEW DIRECTIONS FOR HIGHER EDUCATION • DOI: 10.1002/he

abroad participation rates have long been and continue to be liberal arts colleges (for example, sixteen of the seventeen colleges and universities sending more than 80 percent of graduates abroad in 2006/2007 identified themselves as liberal arts institutions) (Bhandari and Chow, 2008).

Study abroad remains of high value to many liberal arts colleges and to higher education in the United States in general. Nevertheless, at least two factors have contributed to a reevaluation of the study-abroad program's role within international education and educational institutions, including the liberal arts college. First, assumptions about the purpose and nature of study abroad have changed. If study abroad once was associated primarily with the study of modern languages, international studies, and area studies, more recently it has expanded to include virtually all undergraduate majors. This expansion was fueled in part by calls such as Burn's (1990) to allow study abroad to earn credit toward the major. In the past twenty years, the percentage of study-abroad programs taking place in historically underrepresented fields of study has expanded: business and management (from 10.9 to 19.1 percent); health sciences (from 1.7 to 4.2 percent); engineering (from 1.6 to 3.1 percent); and physical and life sciences (from 3.8 to 7.7 percent) (Bhandari and Chow, 2008; Zikopoulos, 1987). However, by 1995 the discussion of study abroad shifted to conceptualizing its purpose as developing intercultural competence (American Council on Education, 1995). Indeed, today, a common understanding in the United States of the purpose of study abroad is its contribution to intercultural and transformational learning (Brewer and Cunningham, 2010; Savicki, 2008).

Second, in the 1990s, particularly in the United States and the European Union, a move toward internationalization took place in higher education. Members of the European Association of International Education (EAIE), concerned about relatively low rates of student and family mobility and the marginal impact of this activity on the content and delivery of education at the home institution, began to reject a reliance on mobility as the vehicle for international education. How were students who did not go abroad being prepared for life in increasingly multicultural societies? Were faculty and institutions equipped to provide an education appropriate to this task? The response was a call for Internationalization at Home, or IaH (Nilsson and Otten, 2003). North American scholars and educational organizations called for a similar internationalization of colleges and universities. Both NAFSA: Association of International Educators and the American Council on Education have done work in this area, the latter drawing on Knight's definition of internationalization "as the process of integrating an international, intercultural, or global dimension into the purpose, functions, or delivery of post-secondary education" (American Council on Education, 2008, p. 2). As with IaH, the idea behind internationalization is to move beyond discrete sets of activities to strategies for institutional transformation. The reevaluation of the purpose and nature of study abroad and its role in internationalization helped Beloit College look toward international partnerships as a way to help internationalize its faculty, and through them, the curriculum.

Beloit College Internationalization Experience: The Role of the Faculty. As noted earlier in this chapter, Beloit College's international involvement began soon after its founding. It accelerated in 1960, when a review of the curriculum resulted in the establishment of a World Affairs Center charged with promoting international education, the addition of new languages and courses in international studies, and the creation of a World Outlook Program of faculty-led study-abroad seminars. In the 1980s and 1990s, the college began shifting away from faculty-led seminars as the primary form of study abroad to exchanges, direct enrollment in universities, and the use of a limited number of third-party provider study-abroad options. The shift was motivated by a desire to offer study-abroad options in more majors, limitations of faculty time to initiate study-abroad seminars or spend a semester abroad, and, in the case of exchanges, a desire to limit the outflow of dollars to support study abroad and to diversify the student body by bringing students from partner universities to campus for one or two semesters. The shift in programming allowed foreign instructors in Spanish and Russian to teach at Beloit College, while Beloit faculty occasionally accompanied students to partner universities as advisors and tutors.

The creation of an administrative unit responsible for study abroad led to many positive results. The number of students studying abroad increased to approximately 45 percent by 2000. Study abroad across the curriculum increased because Beloit College's majors could be accommodated in the curriculum of various universities abroad. Further, the per-student cost of study abroad was kept relatively low because tuition dollars did not leave the campus in the case of exchanges, and a steady stream of students from partner institutions enriched classroom discussions and campus life.

On the other hand, because faculty members were less involved in the education students were receiving while abroad, study-abroad became more distant from their work. Further, as study abroad was, in a sense, outsourced to universities abroad and specialized programs for American students, what study abroad was meant to accomplish became less clear to the campus as a whole, and to the students in particular. Thus, although applications to study abroad had to be approved by a faculty committee, in general the sense was that even if a student exhibited relatively little preparation and planning for study-abroad, she or he nonetheless was bound to get something out of it. It was not completely clear that this assumption was valid (Engle and Engle, 2002). Indeed, some students reported disappointment with their study-abroad experiences. Sometimes this was because they had spent too much time with other Americans; other times their language skills or status as outsider made communication difficult. Students enrolled in universities often found the institutions difficult to negotiate; unused to courses with single assessments at the end of the semester, they did not know how to go about their studies. Those enrolled in programs created for

American students, on the other hand, often complained that the courses were pitched too low if they already had experience in the subject matter.

These challenges do not imply that the same students did not feel they had learned anything; indeed, they often reported they had learned a lot, just not academically. Further, other students found they advanced academically. A student reluctant to study history at Beloit College, for example, reported that in history courses taken abroad, "I learned so much that I didn't just do well on the test. I absorbed so much I could share it with other people. I actually got to see the sights we were talking about, and could use all my senses to really learn something." Another wrote that study abroad showed her how "to think in the interdisciplinary vein. It gave me more to draw on and rounded out lessons I'd already learned by forcing me to put my education into practice" (Beloit College, 2007–2008).

The questions for Beloit College, therefore, became how to recognize when students were learning and why and when they were not and why; how to prepare students better for study abroad and help them build on the experience upon return; and what was the role of the faculty in shaping the study-abroad experience. Beginning in 2000, the college began to discuss how best to integrate study abroad into students' studies. Surveys of Beloit College faculty, students, and staff conducted in 2004 provided evidence that there was strong support for international education and study abroad in particular; however, the curriculum was found somewhat wanting (Beloit College, 2005).

A series of campuswide faculty conversations, begun in 2000, on Beloit College's program of international education resulted in several actions to strengthen it. These included the creation of a mission statement for international education and the identification of learning goals for study abroad, the adoption of a more intentional study-abroad application process, and the visible assessment of study-abroad learning outcomes in the form of a symposium in which students would present lessons from their study abroad. As well, however, the campus asked itself about the international education received by students who neither were studying abroad nor came to the campus from another country. Conversations also took place about the role of the faculty in the delivery of international education and study abroad and the value added to Beloit College through its international partnerships, most of which centered on the exchange of students.

The conclusions eventually reached were that (1) more attention needed to be paid to how the curriculum could prepare students for study abroad and help them bring their study-abroad experiences into dialogue with their ongoing studies upon return; (2) faculty needed opportunities to gain more international experience, better understand the nature of study-abroad, and experiment with pedagogical approaches to strengthen the study-abroad experience; and (3) international partnerships currently were not delivering the best possible educational experience for Beloit College students, but nevertheless could possibly serve as a resource to address the first two concerns. In addressing these issues, a commitment to student mobility would remain, but attention to the work of the faculty and the role of partnerships in advancing internationalization garnered greater attention. This shift would require changing the culture of the institution to achieve long-term impacts (Heyl, 2007).

Internationalization: Investment in Faculty and the Leveraging of Resources. In an article on the role of faculty in internationalization, Stohl (2007) argues that international education offers the opportunity for transformative learning, but that for this learning to take place, faculty members and their scholarship need to be transformed as well. An assessment of internationalization that relies on numbers alone (study abroad and international student enrollments, courses with international content, countries represented in the curriculum and in the faculty, international partnerships) will fail to get at the purpose and meaningful outcomes of internationalization. Stohl asserts that to achieve more robust results, institutions need to understand how internationalization contributes to learning, and for that, the role of the faculty is crucial. Similarly, others have argued that if a college or university president has money for nothing else toward internationalization, the money should be invested in the faculty, and that faculty development needs to be grounded in "faculty ownership, choice, and support," integrated with "other internationalization strategies," and be extended to an ever-expanding "circle of engaged faculty" (Green and Olson, 2003, p. 78).

Collegewide conversations helped Beloit College identify the need for greater faculty involvement in international education. Initial steps were to expand the mandate of the faculty oversight committee for international education to include responsibility for helping to advance the college's internationalization. Committee members serve for two years, and this rotation serves as a vehicle for bringing an ever-expanding circle of faculty into discussions of international education. Other vehicles for faculty international development have been site visits to Beloit's international partners and selected programs run by other organizations. Sometimes small groups of faculty members travel together, although faculty visiting third-party provider programs often do so as part of a delegation whose members come from a number of different institutions. The main outcomes of such visits tends to be a better understanding of learning opportunities for students and the employ of these to convey the opportunities to the campus through advising, displays in departments, and participation in an off-campus study fair. Some faculty, however, use the visits to incorporate the host country into their teaching and scholarship.

Even though visits to study-abroad sites are worthwhile, they are not sufficient in themselves for internationalizing the curriculum. In recognition of this, the College's central faculty development fund has encouraged international engagement. Several faculty members have been able to take advantage of this funding to undertake activities connecting their teaching to the site; dance faculty, for example, found productive opportunities in Moscow. Other faculty have applied the funds toward the cost of participation in Council on International Educational Exchange (CIEE) faculty development seminars to reshape or develop courses. The College's participation in Global Partners, a consortia partnership of the Associated Colleges of the Midwest, the Colleges of the South, and the Great Lakes Colleges Association, offered similar faculty development opportunities, allowing Beloit College to bring two Fulbright Scholars-in-Residence to campus to help internationalize the gender studies curriculum as well as interdisciplinary health courses.

The most transformational international faculty development activities to date at Beloit College, however, have involved faculty meeting together, in Beloit as well as in study-abroad sites, to advance the curriculum and embed study abroad within it. In 2003, for example, an ad hoc group of faculty members concerned about the learning outcomes from study abroad convened over several weeks to discuss the creation of pre- and post-study-abroad courses. Two in the group then participated in the College's summer interdisciplinary workshop to develop learning goals and syllabi for the courses. Consistent with research findings on the nature of intercultural competency (Deardorff, 2008), the pre-study-abroad course subsequently aimed to help students understand concrete and abstract differences between the U.S. and their intended host countries, develop the ability to recognize, analyze, and understand multiple perspectives, and negotiate different modes of communication. The post-study-abroad course sought to help students understand their own assumptions and values, and how their study-abroad experiences related to their intellectual and personal education. These courses continue to be taught today.

To truly transform the curriculum, however, it is important to get at the work faculty do in their everyday teaching, and to transform the institution, to find connections to others who participate in creating and delivering the curriculum. Due to the new campus perspectives on international work, faculty members interested in internationalizing the curriculum and strengthening the study-abroad experience took advantage of a Beloit College presidential initiative to foster innovation to apply for funding for a workshop on integrating study abroad into the curriculum that would focus on the locations of its partners. Funding from the presidential initiative supported the participation of representatives from two international partners where Beloit hoped to strengthen the experience of its students. Applicants to the workshop, organized around the theme of Cities in Transition, were asked to discuss how the workshop would enhance their teaching.

Ultimately, the week-long workshop, held on the Beloit College campus and using the city of Beloit as a laboratory, resulted in the introduction of courses on Dakar in Transition and Quito in Transition, taught by local faculty in the respective cities, and a substantial reworking of a similar course taught in China. The latter is taught largely as a distance-learning course by a Beloit faculty member, as is a course on Moscow in Transition, for which initial ideas were gathered in the same workshop, and further developed in subsequent workshops at Beloit's partner university in Moscow and again in Beloit. Some of the faculty involved in the workshops had previously participated in a seminar and site visit to China to understand the environment, but also to incorporate teaching about China into courses outside of the Asian Studies program. Others had visited Beloit College's partners in Ecuador and Senegal, with the same intentions. Participants in these visits subsequently incorporated the target countries into their teaching, whether in language and culture courses, gender and women's studies, medical anthropology, interdisciplinary courses, or first-year seminars. One faculty member used these faculty development activities to create a course examining the relationship between health and poverty in Nicaragua and Beloit. Discussions of some of these examples can be found in a volume on *Integrating Study Abroad into the Curriculum: Theory and Practice Across the Disciplines* (Brewer and Cunningham, 2010).

Critical to the curricular outcomes of these faculty development activities was a focus on how learning outside the classroom takes place, the particular challenges and opportunities for this learning in study-abroad sites, and how partnerships and other resources can be leveraged to support faculty and curriculum development. Visits to Beloit College partners' institutions and explorations of the cities in which they are located have been invaluable in helping faculty understand the context for their students' study-abroad experiences and the challenges they face in learning. This perspective helps faculty see how their own teaching might better prepare students for their experiences, and how their advising and teaching can help them build on their experiences when they return to campus. Equally important has been providing space and time for faculty members from different disciplines to discuss how learning abroad takes place and to experiment with different pedagogical approaches to encourage experiential and intercultural learning.

The faculty development activities described here could not have been successful had they not been embedded in a larger project or process of changing the way Beloit College had thought about study abroad and its relationship to the curriculum, its mission, and the work of the faculty. In its first attempts at study abroad, programs belonged to the faculty who led particular seminars that traveled abroad. Later, study abroad was largely outsourced to universities and study-abroad organizations. In this latest phase, study abroad is seen as an activity that can enhance the education taking place on campus if students can be asked to find ways to connect it to their ongoing studies and faculty can not only understand the study-abroad experience, but use it to change the pedagogy they employ. Evidence of the success of this approach can be found in the college's decision to employ pedagogical approaches from the Cities in Transition project in the first-year seminars taken by all entering students, with implementation scheduled for fall 2010. The following case study will discuss this development as well as benefits accrued to both parties to an institutional partnership.

Case Study: The Beloit College–Henan University Partnership

In 2005, Beloit College was in search of a new university partner in China. Priority was for a university in a Mandarin-speaking area so that Beloit's students of Chinese language could advance their language skills. The ideal partner would have a good program of Chinese as a foreign language, relatively few American students, be receptive to the exchange of undergraduate students, and have an international office able to assume responsibility for implementation of the partnership. The college's experience with foreign universities with significant populations of U.S. and other "Western" students was that it was easy for students to be caught up in an expatriate student community and fail to engage with local people and environments. As well, the college was mindful that a partnership with a liberal arts college may not be attractive to a Chinese university seeking to link based on prestige. Further, some of Beloit College's past partnerships had been difficult to operationalize because of the lack of infrastructure to support the relationship.

Another impulse, however, was to find a partner receptive to the idea of creating a course for Beloit College that would intentionally require Beloit College students' engagement with people and environments beyond the university campus. This course in turn would require opportunities for Beloit faculty to visit the partner to better understand the environment for study abroad and to experiment with pedagogy. Twenty-five years of experience with institutional partnerships had demonstrated that Beloit College needed to take responsibility for creating opportunities for its students to grow intellectually and personally when they studied abroad. Although advocates of international exchanges have argued that immersion in a foreign university offer the most robust learning environment (Carlson, Burn, Useem, and Yachimowicz, 1990), Beloit College had found that pedagogical differences were often disruptive to the learning process. As a learner-centered college with highly structured classes and assignments, it was wrong to assume that its students would be able to thrive when thrust into classrooms with knowledge- and faculty-centered pedagogical approaches. Current critiques of direct enrollment in universities abroad (Vande Berg, 2007) argue that a structured program can promise better learning for study-abroad. This kind of learning requires preparation and intervention throughout the study-abroad experience (Vande Berg, 2007), the development of intercultural skills and behaviors, and opportunities to learn experientially, including through reflection (Bennett, 2008). It was neither appropriate nor possible, however, to ask existing and potential partner institutions to both change their pedagogical approach *and* provide the supports for this kind of resource-intensive instruction. In essence, Beloit College was seeking opportunities to form a bridge between immersion in another university and the structured interventions common to many study-abroad programs today. The College, therefore, sought a partner hospitable to admitting Beloit students to its Chinese language program, receptive to visits from Beloit faculty, open to adding a course to its students' schedules that would teach them to learn experientially and interculturally, and amendable to sending its undergraduates to Beloit College for either one or two semesters.

Research on Chinese universities led to the identification of Henan University in Kaifeng, Henan Province, as a potential partner. Founded in 1912 to prepare students for further study in Europe and the United States, the university appeared to meet the basic criteria outlined above by Beloit College. Subsequent to a positive response from the Henan University international office, a faculty member in the Chinese program charged by the college to help secure a new partnership, and myself, the director of International Education, traveled to Kaifeng in March 2006. There we visited Chinese language classes, toured the university facilities, and met with university officials. On our own, we explored the city of Kaifeng to gather ideas as to how the city might serve as the "text" for one of the Cities in Transition courses described elsewhere in this chapter. Henan University's senior officials as well as Mr. Ma Xiaoyang, head of the international office, were hospitable to the notion of forming a partnership. Initially, they preferred to send junior faculty to Beloit so that they could spend time in an English-speaking country. Ultimately, however, they agreed that undergraduates were more suited to Beloit because the college could not support the needs of junior faculty. As a side note, Henan University inquired as to the possibility of Beloit sending graduates, ideally with training in teaching English as a foreign language, to Henan University as English teachers. Although this did not become a formal part of the agreement, in fact from the start it has been a productive component of the partnership for both institutions.

In 2006/2007, Beloit College and Henan University exchanged their first students and three Beloit May 2006 graduates were invited to teach English in Kaifeng. Funding from a Freeman Foundation grant allowed several faculty members, both within and outside Asian studies, to visit Henan University in October 2006 to explore connections to their work and to see the context for the Chinese Cities in Transition course. As well, the visit gave the two institutions an opportunity to evaluate the current activity. A formal cooperation agreement subsequently was concluded, with a signing ceremony taking place in Kaifeng in May 2007, attended by faculty and top officials from both institutions. A Henan University delegation visited Beloit College in November 2008, with two Beloit faculty members lecturing at Henan University in spring 2009 while on sabbatical in Beijing. A faculty member in sociology and Beloit College's new dean visited Henan University in summer 2009.

NEW DIRECTIONS FOR HIGHER EDUCATION • DOI: 10.1002/he

These visits have served as an investment in the relationship on the part of the two institutions. For Beloit College, the visits have led to curricular connections and the creation of a sense of faculty ownership of the partnership. Beloit faculty have developed courses due to their visits, expanded rotation as instructors in the Chinese Cities in Transition, and brought pedagogy developed in visits to Kaifeng into first-year seminars. The impact on Beloit College students studying at Henan University has been similarly robust. The ethnographic research projects they have conducted in Kaifeng—for example, on night markets, a Halal restaurant, and a Catholic church and its hospice—have stretched them linguistically, culturally, intellectually, and personally. The projects and their studies at the university have allowed them to truly engage with local people and environments and change their own perspectives and assumptions.

Henan University also has seen impacts on its teaching. According to Ma Xiaoyang, Beloit College students are helping "Henan students understand American culture and people," while the Beloit graduates serving as English teachers "not only have . . . brought with them a completely new method of teaching, they have also demonstrated to the younger faculty at Henan University new pedagogies [and] have helped their students and our teachers to raise their abilities to study and use English" (Ma Xiaoyang, personal communication, November 30, 2009). The Henan University students coming to Beloit, in turn, have been able to experience "a high quality education in the area of their major," "open up their eyes to the world," and "gain more experiences in human life" (Ma Xiaoyang, personal communication, November 30, 2009).

The lessons both institutions take from the partnership are that its success has rested on the careful selection of student participants and stewardship of the partnership by the respective international offices. Further, the visits by faculty and officials have been a vehicle for both deepening commitment to the partnership and opening up new possibilities for cooperation. Henan University, for example, would like to host more Beloit College faculty for lectures and discussions with its faculty members. In spring 2010, Beloit College will host the Henan University staff member responsible for day-to-day implementation of the partnership for the semester. He will audit classes, assist with various projects, and serve as a teaching assistant in Chinese. Though the two institutions differ in size and educational approach, both share an international outlook. Because Henan University "has always valued [. . .] connections abroad" it was open to a partnership with Beloit College, no matter its ranking and size (Ma Xiaoyang, personal communication, November 30, 2009).

This case study makes clear that the success of the Beloit College–Henan University relationship has been made possible through a commitment of human resources throughout the institutions. Though actual numbers of involved students are small, the curricular impacts for both institutions have been greater than anticipated, in part through the presence at Henan University of Beloit graduates as English teachers. This experience exemplifies putting a liberal education into practice. As one of the teachers writes, "Teaching at Henan University has been more of a learning experience than a job. Every day I learn something new. [The] experience helps me to review all the ideas and assumptions I had developed in my . . . education [at Beloit] (Hansen, personal communication, November 30, 2009). The teacher's experience provides an assessment of the outcomes of liberal education.

References

American Council on Education. *Educating Americans for a World in Flux: Ten Ground Rules for Internationalizing American Higher Education.* Washington, D.C.: American Council on Education, 1995.

Association of American Colleges and Universities (AAC&U). "What Is Liberal Education?," 2009a. Retrieved November 25, 2009, from http://www.aacu.org/leap/What_is_liberal_education.cfm

Association of American Colleges and Universities (AAC&U). "America's Promise: Liberal Education and America's Promise (LEAP)," 2009b. Retrieved December 1, 2009, from http://www.aacu.org/leap/vision.cfm

Beloit College. "Self Study of International Education." Unpublished document, Beloit College, Beloit, Wis., 2005.

Beloit College. Study abroad evaluations. Unpublished document, Office of International Education files, Beloit College, Beloit, Wis., 2007–2008.

Bennett, J. "On Becoming a Global Soul: A Path to Engagement During Study Abroad." In V. Savicki (ed.), *Developing Intercultural Competence and Transformation: Theory, Research, and Application in International Education.* Sterling, Va.: Stylus, 2008.

Bhandari, R., and Chow, P. *Open Doors 2008: Report on International Educational Exchange.* New York: Institute of International Education, 2008.

Brewer, E., and Cunningham, K. (eds.). *Integrating Study Abroad into the Curriculum: Theory and Practice Across the Disciplines.* Sterling, Va.: Stylus, 2010.

Burn, B. B. *The Contribution of International Educational Exchange to the International Education of Americans: Projections for the Year 2000.* Occasional Papers on International Educational Exchange 26. New York: Council on International Educational Exchange, 1990.

Carlson, J. S., Burn, B. B., Useem, J., and Yachimovicz, D. *Study Abroad: The Experience of American Undergraduates.* Westport, CT: Greenwood, 1990.

Commission on the Abraham Lincoln Study Abroad Fellowship Program. *Global Competence and National Needs: One Million Americans Studying Abroad.* Washington, D.C.: NAFSA, 2007.

Committee of the Yale College Corporation and the Faculty. "The Yale Report of 1828, Part I, 1828." In *The Collegiate Way: Residential Colleges & the Renewal of University Life.* Retrieved December 4, 2009, from http://collegiateway.org/reading/yale-report-1828/

Deardorff, D. K. "Intercultural Competence: A Definition, Model, and Implications for Education Abroad." In V. Savicki (ed.), *Developing Intercultural Competence and Transformation: Theory, Research, and Application in International Education.* Sterling, Va.: Stylus, 2008.

Engle, J., and Engle, L. "Neither International nor Educative: Study Abroad in the Time of Globalization." In W. Grünzweig and N. Rinehart (eds.), *Rockin' in Red Square: Critical Approaches to International Education in the Age of Cyberculture.* Münster, Germany: LIT, 2002.

Gore, J. E. *Dominant Beliefs and Alternative Voices: Discourse, Belief, and Gender in American Study Abroad.* New York: Routledge, 2005.

Green, M. F., and Olson, C. *Internationalizing the Campus: A User's Guide.* Washington, D.C.: American Council on Education, Center for Institutional and International Initiatives, 2003.

Heyl, J. *The Senior International Officer (SIO) as Change Agent.* Durham, N.C.: Association of International Education Administrators, 2007.

Hoffa, W. W. *A History of U.S. Study Abroad: Beginnings to 1965.* Carlisle, Pa.: The Forum on Education Abroad, Dickinson College, 2007.

Julius, D. J. "3 Key Issues in Exchanges with China." *Chronicle of Higher Education,* August 31, 2009. Retrieved August 31, 2009 from http://chronicle.com/article/Due-Diligence-for-Exchanges/48222/?sid=at&utm_source=at&utm_medium=en

Kehm, B. H. "Germany: The Quest for World-Class Universities." *International Higher Education,* 2009, *54,* 18–20.

Nilsson, B., and Otten, M. (eds.). "Internationalisation at Home." *Journal of Studies in International Education,* 2003, *7*(1) (entire issue).

Nussbaum, M. *Cultivating Humanity and World Citizenship.* Cambridge, Mass.: Forum for the Future of Higher Education, 2007. Retrieved November 23, 2009, from http://net.educause.edu/ir/library/pdf/ff0709s.pdf

Tillman, M. J. (ed.). *Cooperating with a University in the United States: NAFSA's Guide to Interuniversity Linkages.* Washington, D.C.: NAFSA: Association of International Educators, 2007.

Savicki, V. (ed.). *Developing Intercultural Competence and Transformation: Theory, Research, and Application in International Education.* Sterling, Va.: Stylus, 2008.

Siegel, K. (ed.). *No Longer the College on the Hill: Beloit's International Outlook from 1947–1924.* Beloit, Wis.: Beloit College Archives, 1992.

Stohl, M. "We Have Met the Enemy and He Is Us: The Role of the Faculty in the Internationalization of Higher Education in the Coming Decade." *Journal of Studies in International Education,* 2007, *11*(3/4), 359–372.

Vande Berg, M. "Intervening in the Learning of U.S. Students Abroad." *Journal of Studies in International Education,* 2007, *11*(3/4), 392–399.

Zikopoulos, M. (ed.). *Open Doors: 1986/87 Report on International Educational Exchange.* New York: Institute of International Education, 1987.

ELIZABETH BREWER *is director of international education at Beloit College, Wisconsin.*

8

Student expectations and experiences of studying abroad have changed due to a number of factors including global politics, job markets, faculty advisement, and use of the Internet.

Student Learning in an International Setting

Darren Kelly

This chapter explores student learning in an international setting and the importance that students place on the international setting when they are considering where to study abroad. It examines how the social distance of foreign sites from America has been reduced in recent years due to globalization, politics, the Internet, internationalization of the curriculum, and the value the job market places on global competency. In my discussion, I draw upon recent research I completed with forty-five American students studying in Ireland with the study-abroad provider Institute for the International Education of Students (IES) in the summer and fall semesters of 2009. As part of that research, the students kept a daily record of the time, duration, and mode of their communication with home occurring predominantly via e-mail, Facebook, and Skype. The fall student sample also completed a survey, which illustrated the reasons they chose to study abroad, and the role played by their faculty advisors in the decision-making process.

This chapter illustrates how trends in student expectations and experiences of study-abroad are challenging the cross-border collaborations of universities and study-abroad providers to match these expectations with relevant academic and cultural experiences. Concepts discussed in this chapter are connected to the work I have completed with the Office of International Education of Beloit College, which has been funded by the Fulbright Commission and the Andrew W. Mellon Foundation.

New Directions for Higher Education, no. 150, Summer 2010 © Wiley Periodicals, Inc.
Published online in Wiley InterScience (www.interscience.wiley.com) • DOI: 10.1002/he.393

Introduction: Setting the Scene

Italo Calvino in *Invisible Cities* (1997) rhetorically argues that perceived differences between countries are best preserved by looking at an atlas. One can imagine that the large tracts of water, topography, and the bold lines that act as political borders, aid one's notions of geographic and cultural differences. Why? Because once in situ Calvino claims the differences, particularly over time, become erased to the extent that "only the name of the airport changes" (Calvino, 1997, p. 128).

Calvino's fiction, originally published in the 1960s, was ahead of its time, as it entertained visions of what are more contemporaneously described as globalized and postmodern spaces. As such, it can be applied to some students' choices for studying abroad; from the students' perspectives, the farther away and more exotic the location the better (Woolf, 2006). Deresiewicz (2009) adds that partially due to its perceived similarities with America, Europe is less attractive for students:

> Travel is an idea about our relationship to the world: what kinds of experiences we expect from it, what we think it has to teach us, how we map it in our heads. The world has changed, and Americans have changed—it's no surprise that the way that young Americans set out to court the world has also changed. (¶1)

For Deresiewicz (2009), the setting for international education matters for students, with mystique, family heritage, liberal guilt, and future employment prospects listed as students' reasons for choosing to study in non-Western countries. When linked to Calvino's (1997) comment on the similarity of places, a case can be made that when U.S. students study in countries that are deemed culturally similar to their own—for example, Europe—the similarities of the two countries can teach students more about themselves and where they come from than the socially distanced mystique of "truly" foreign countries. (Of course, when in those countries, students can learn to see that many of them have been affected by globalization, and thus now share similarities when one looks beyond the veil of difference.) As Calvino (1997) writes, "You take delight not in a city's seven or seventy wonders, but in the answer it gives to a question of yours. . . .Or the question it asks you, forcing you to answer, like Thebes through the mouth of the Sphinx" (p. 44). The new context puts in relief students' assumptions about the United States and themselves.

Despite location as the primary reason for some students' choice of a study-abroad program, in reality most inhabit more than one location while abroad. Contemporary students' increasing use of social network sites such as Facebook and Skype compress time and space so that students are operating in a form of ambi-location, which is living in one place while operating co-terminously in a different space. For example, my research on students studying in Ireland reveals that many are connected to America via the Internet for more than 2 hours each evening; this is also the case with students I have interacted with in China, Ecuador, and Russia. As well as connecting (plugging in) with home via the Internet, students throughout the day are thinking about, and dealing with, issues connected to home. The issue of student Internet usage and the attendant physical and emotional withdrawing from the host culture poses interesting philosophical questions concerning study-abroad students' perceptions of community, time, and space, as well as links to discourse on society and space in geography, philosophy, and sociology (Auge, 1995; Bauman, 2000; Dear, 2000; Foucault, 1986; Harvey, 1990; Lefebvre, 1994; Sennett, 1974; Soja, 1989).

Making students aware of their Internet usage and analyzing their everyday modus operandi through the context of academic disciplines and theory is one example of how students can benefit personally through self-reflexivity while at the same time gaining an understanding of the sometimes complex study of theory and critical thinking. This pedagogy fits into the broader discussion of interdisciplinary learning and curriculum integration (Beane, 1997; Gore, 2005; McBrien and Brandt, 1997).

Divergent Views on the Benefits of Studying Abroad

Motivations and objectives for student participation in study abroad vary. Pablo Toral (2010) argues institutions take a utilitarian approach that aims to foster student skill sets that will engender "more productive workers who will be able to develop competitive firms in the age of globalization" (p. 191). Edwards (2000) provides a counterpoint to this view as she argues students and their parents take a developmental approach to study-abroad, which focuses on individual self-maturation and attainment of greater self-confidence.

Having taught American undergraduates in Ireland and developed customized programs for a range of American institutions and study-abroad providers, I believe both of these viewpoints are present and cause tensions between students, parents, faculty, and administrators. For example, in the survey research discussed in this chapter, only one student cited developing expertise in an academic major as a reason for studying abroad. The majority expressed various forms of "individual self-maturation" as the primary reason; studying country-specific courses was secondary and, for many, these courses were not specifically related to their major or minor.

Academic institutions need to ensure that students consider the importance of taking the "study element" of going abroad seriously and make them aware of the programs that provide course choices that best match their major and minor. Institutions also need to collaborate with faculty to consider the potential for internationalizing their curricula, and with study-abroad providers to explore ways in which academic courses can incorporate elements of, for example, intercultural competency.

NEW DIRECTIONS FOR HIGHER EDUCATION • DOI: 10.1002/he

Selby (2008) argues that students expect "life-changing" experiences whereas faculty (and institutional criteria) want the students' time to mirror and fulfill home campus curriculum needs, adding "learning, at this level, is linked to a familiar didactic process with the same evaluation procedures used on campus. In fact, any deviation from traditional *academic* practice is viewed askance, with suspicion" (p. 1). Overt educational differences between U.S. and foreign institutions' educational structures, and philosophies can cause tensions in cross-border collaborations based on differences such as class size, course delivery (lecture versus discussion), course prerequisites, size of reading lists, level of student feedback, and weighting of grades.

This nexus in the student learning experience is an area where collaboration between study-abroad providers and the home campus is essential. A home institution imposing intellectual and academic trades and tariffs on study-abroad providers simply replicates the course content and pedagogy of the home campus. As a result, students will not have the chance to learn differently and think differently about the content and delivery of education; it also decreases their understanding of how different cultural groups acquire and disseminate knowledge.

Bennett (2008) strongly argues a need for students to be interculturally and internationally competent and intellectually adaptable. In support of his claims, he references research in international education (Mestenhauser and Ellingboe, 1998) and celebrates the increasing disciplinary range in research across the academy that focuses on the value of international education and its cultural context (Cornwell and Stoddard, 1999, 2001; Deardorff, 2005, 2006; Hovland, 2006; Meacham and Gaff, 2006). The Lincoln Commission (Supreme Court, 2003, as cited in Bennett, 2008) stated, "What nations don't know can hurt them. The stakes in study abroad are that simple, that straight forward, and that important. For their own future and that of the nation, college graduates today must be that internationally competent" (pp. 13–14). An argument can be made that the utilitarian and developmental views of study abroad outlined above represent a false dichotomy because a range of academic disciplines provide ample conceptual frameworks and theories with which the intercultural and transformational aspect of the students' desires for study abroad (campus field work and service learning) can be accommodated; as Selby (2008) claims, "International educators all too often leave it to serendipity to bridge [them]" (p. 3).

The desire for students to gain international experiences is clear, but as outlined above, institutional and curricular barriers exist. One dominant barrier is the lack of faculty knowledge of and/or reservations about the value of study abroad (Brewer and Cunningham, 2010). In marked contrast to the importance given to international education and study abroad (Bennett, 2008; Mestenhauser, 1998; Peterson, 2000; Stohl, 2007), almost three quarters of the students I surveyed responded that their advisors ranged from being blasé about study abroad to actively discouraging them from studying abroad. One faculty member explicitly advised a student not to take a class in his major discipline while abroad. Brewer and Cunningham (2010) thus advocate for the creation of faculty development programs that encourage faculty to learn about study abroad in general and specific programs aligned with their scholarly activities and teaching. They also recommend programs that allow faculty to study and conduct research abroad, and posit that these activities can increase the internationalization of the campus and curriculum.

Student Experiences and Expectations of Study Abroad

This section provides a chronological account of some radical changes in American students' experiences and expectations of study abroad, and how these expectations challenge cross-border collaboration and curriculum provision. Students' experiences of study abroad can be broadly summarized as a traditional desire to experience a "foreign" culture different from the United States to a different engagement and perspective of the United States in the study-abroad site. Finally, in a reversal of the "getting away from it all" mentality, students' use of the Internet has resulted in their being ambi-located between the host society and the United States.

Getting Away from It All. Traditionally, study abroad has been based on the concept of the full immersion of students in a foreign setting for an extended period of time, preferably one year (Hoffa, 2007). This format of study abroad is analogous to the expression being "thrown in at the deep end," where students learn to physically and socio-culturally navigate (swim) in the host society through the development of their foreign language and interpersonal skills. The full immersion process can lead to an initial feeling of culture shock and anxiety that, in the past, was exacerbated by the expense of telephone calls and the time lag between letters.

Students can cure their homesickness by learning how to engage with and comfortably inhabit their new settings, partially by normalizing the host culture (Allport, 1964). This process of learning to connect with new places and temper desires for home is a valuable tool that enables students to be confident travelers, and to adapt quickly when moving to new places for employment after graduation.

Although learning to cope with the new and different is valuable, it might, by association, prevent students from connecting what they see (socio-economics, culture, and politics) with home. This kind of social and emotional distancing of experience with the self and home links with discourse, particularly in anthropology, that argues research and study can be commodified and self-serving, and become more akin to well-intentioned, but sometimes questionable eco-tourism, than a rigorous engagement with and analysis of the host culture that requires cultural sensitivity and self-reflexivity (Bruner, 2005). The danger of unintentionally turning study abroad into quasi-academic tourism is a particular risk for short-term intensive study-abroad programs.

Brewer and Cunningham (2010) argue that students returning from study abroad have felt dislocated on campus due to a lack of interpersonal and academic outlets. Post-study-abroad academic courses can offer fertile ground for students to develop their international experiences and lead to graduate research and employment (Toral, 2010) and places international education within the continuum of a student's time at college (Bennett, 2008).

Coming Face-to-Face with Themselves on Foreign Soil. It has been out of necessity, rather than design, that some students have increasingly come face-to-face with and been challenged by home when abroad. Eight years ago, I began teaching a course on Irish culture and identity to American undergraduates in Ireland. I considered American identity to be an important frame of reference; however, some students did not feel particularly comfortable or willing to discuss this. Issues ranging from abortion to the 9/11 terrorist attack and immigration were too personal and regarded as dangerous territory to enter. Discussing Ireland was safer because it was "other."

America's involvement in the second Gulf War in 2003 led to an immediate analysis of its foreign policy on a global scale through vast television networks and the Internet. American students studying abroad were soon engaged in debates with members of their host countries about these issues and students, even in very pro-American countries such as Ireland, were faced with anti-American sentiment. The reaction by students in my class varied. Some mistook opposing views and debates of American policy as a personal slight or attack, whereas others believed that to argue against their president at a time of war was unpatriotic. According to the American study-abroad organization Council on International Educational Exchange (CIEE; 2009), American students are "ill-prepared to serve as informal diplomats for the U.S. or even understand that they might have that role. And, when confronted by hostility abroad, they are simply dumbfounded about how anyone could feel that way about them" (CIEE, 2009, ¶5). To aid the students' abilities to critically evaluate different cultural contexts on issues, and develop an ability to articulate their own views, CIEE (2009) recommends that "[a] required cross-cultural learning course or segment should exist in every study abroad program. Study abroad is about cross-cultural competence and it doesn't happen by osmosis" (CIEE, 2009, ¶10).

The willingness of students to engage in more open discussion changed in part due to the presidential debates in 2004 between President George Bush and Senator John Kerry because opposing viewpoints of American policy became increasingly normalized in American public spheres. More recently, the increasing internationalization of college curricula and the positivity engendered by President Obama has enabled at least some students to feel more confident about discussing politics in their study-abroad site. Ultimately, students traveling abroad are partially on a voyage of discovery about where they have come from.

The Value of Study Abroad. In my survey of students, one rationale students provided for studying abroad was that the intercultural competence and global knowledge they gained would benefit their graduate applications and education and job prospects. These links are evidenced by the increasing number of study-abroad alumni who are requesting letters of recommendation from their study-abroad professors at IES in Ireland to aid their applications for graduate school. Students are increasingly choosing study-abroad courses in business and communication and programs that provide internships.

According to the Supreme Court (2003, as quoted in Bennett, 2008), "Today's global marketplace and the increasing diversity in the American population demand that cross-cultural experience and understanding [is] gained from education" (p. 2). To be successful in understanding the intricacies and vagaries of foreign markets and their consumers, students need to have intellectual adaptability and the cultural skills that are essential for the success of international business collaboration (Bauman, 2000; Bennett, 2008).

The concept of industry influencing Higher Education Institutions (HEIs) and national education policy is not new, nor is the debate concerning the distribution of funding from industry and government across the campus to develop new knowledge technology (Glasson, 2003; Jones-Evans, 2000; Trooboff, Vande Berg, and Rayman, 2007–2008). What is new is the fact that industry and institutions have the potential to put pressure, partially through consumer student demand, on faculty to adapt courses in the social sciences, arts, and humanities to match global marketplace needs in terms of the intercultural and interpersonal skills outlined above.

Time–Space Compression and Ambi-Location

My research completed with American students during the 2009 summer and fall semesters in Ireland found that the highest daily average of time spent on the Internet by a student was 3 hours 44 minutes; 16 minutes was the lowest daily average. It was not unusual for students to periodically spend upwards of 5 hours on the Internet on a given day. Although 16 minutes per day seems quite short, the student in question said this time primarily represented a mandatory daily Skype call to his parents to let them know everything was okay. Thus, helicopter parents have become a dominant variable in the students' daily routine while studying abroad. Having available information and a point of contact for parents should be a vital component of university and study-abroad organizations programs.

Communicating with parents and family was the overwhelming reason for students using Skype, which accounted for 15 percent of their Internet usage; Facebook and general Internet use accounted for 46 percent of their time, whereas e-mail represented 39 percent of their Internet time. Issues that arise from the research include the late nights students spend on the Internet due to the time difference between Ireland and America, which has the potential to render students ineffective during school time. The use of Facebook to communicate with friends is almost done instantaneously, leaving little or no time for students to contemplate and process their experiences. In essence, a portion of each student's day is spent communicating and thus being ambi-located with America.

Students wrote responses to their communication diaries during the research. According to one student, "The quick, easy link to familiarity and home serves as a safety net. It is unlikely that I feel homesick when my family is a few clicks away, but I fear that how convenient it is to connect detracts from the experience of cultural immersion, the essential reason for study abroad." Another student wrote, "Even though I am abroad, I do not want to get lost on what is going on at home with my friends and family. For that reason, I try to keep up with my friends and family as much as I can." A majority of students felt that "checking-in" with home made them more comfortable in their surroundings and warded off or diluted homesickness. Avoiding homesickness, and associated feelings of being lost and dislocated, might prevent students from learning how to situate themselves fully into a new environment and how to become emotionally self-reliant in a foreign setting. Students felt disoriented when they lost their Internet connections due to technical difficulties. Recent research suggests that students can become addicted to the Internet with dire consequences such as dropping out from school and withdrawing from society (Osuagwu, 2009; Zaslow, 2009). Other research suggests that the increasing physical and socio-cultural segregation of people adversely affects society (Davis, 1998; Sennett, 1974; Zukin, 1991).

One student sums up the potential for the misuse of the Internet to dilute the study-abroad experience when she wrote,

> As I look over my communications diary I have come to the conclusion that I have spent too much time on the Internet and Facebook while in Ireland this summer. . . .I lost thirty-eight hours that I could have spent discovering Dublin. Over the past few days I have felt an overwhelming sense of remorse. . . .I see that time as a wasted weekend trip. . . .I sit here now grasping for any reasonable explanation for the ridiculous amount of time that I have wasted. . . .I can't think of anything that can vindicate it.

This ambi-location, or new modus operandi for living (at home and) abroad, has the very real potential to render full-immersion study abroad obsolete, and as a result, change the ways in which universities and study-abroad providers consider their aims and objectives for their programs. Although at first this notion of ambi-location can be seen as a negative duality that dilutes students' engagement with their temporary study-abroad homes, the time–space compression can be used to connect students with their home universities in real-time to collaborate with their professors and peers. The use of Skype can also act as a means for students to engage their relatives and friends at home in the study-abroad experience, which can potentially create a form of trickle-up transformational learning. This might be particularly the case for some first-generation university students and first-generation travelers, whose parents have never had the opportunity to study abroad and/or travel.

Beloit College students studying abroad can take a Beloit International Relations class by connecting into the class through Skype. Reporting on this experience, Jellet, Toral, and Zipse (2009) noted that the study-abroad students could not avoid considering the local context of their study-abroad site when critiquing the class material. Although this benefited and at times interrupted the flow of the class, it clearly illustrates how study-abroad can foster students' better understanding and uses of their academic disciplines and, importantly, challenge assumptions and prejudices students may have about their disciplines.

Conclusion

Student experiences and expectations of study abroad have changed over time. Rather than choosing a study-abroad location based on its perceived difference from America, students increasingly value a study-abroad program's potential for transformative learning. They are also aware of the value intercultural competency, intellectual adaptability, and global competency add to their resumes.

Collaborations between American institutions and their study-abroad partners should include an awareness aware of, and sensitivity towards, the different cultural contexts in education (including philosophical and pedagogical orientations) when developing both national and international curricula and programs. Collaborators also need to be aware of, and possibly adapt, their course offerings to incorporate student-desired outcomes for study abroad, particularly in the area of personal maturation. It has been argued that the personal and academic needs of students need not be separated. However, some faculty are wary of external pressure on curriculum development in general and some faculty are ill-informed and wary of study abroad. However, faculty need to play a central role in the success of study abroad and international education on campus. To encourage these roles, Brewer and Cunningham (2010) strongly recommend the development of faculty development programs to achieve these aims.

As campuses work to expand student experiences abroad, developers should account for the ways student use the Internet. Although students wish to gain intercultural competencies, their extended use of the Internet can greatly reduce their engagement with the host society. To counteract this and to develop intercultural competencies, academic and cultural programs should explicitly include field work and on-site learning in the host country. For example, the presence of large multinationals such as McDonald's can be used as a means for students to investigate the local cultural context of these sites and to encourage a level of self-reflexiveness in student learning, so that they can engage in a voyage of discovery of both home and abroad. Embedding real engagement within the host country can move students beyond superficial learning and provide a reason to get off-line.

References

Allport, G. *The Nature of Prejudice*. Garden City, N.Y.: Doubleday, 1964.

Augé, M. *Non-Lieux, Introduction à une anthropologie de la surmodernité* [*Non-Places: Introduction to an Anthropology of Supermodernity*]. (J. Howe, trans.). London: Verso, 1995.

Bauman, Z. *Liquid Modernity*. Cambridge: Blackwell, 2000.

Beane, J. *Curriculum Integration*. New York: Teachers College, 1997.

Bennett, J. "On Becoming a Global Soul: A Path to Engagement During Study Abroad." In V. Savicki (ed.), *Developing Intercultural Competence and Transformation: Theory, Research, and Application in International Education*. Sterling, Va.: Stylus, 2008.

Brewer, B., and Cunningham, K. "Introduction." In B. Brewer and K. Cunningham (eds.), *Integrating Study Abroad into the Curriculum: Theory and Practice Across the Disciplines*. Sterling, Va.: Stylus, 2010.

Bruner, E. M. *Culture on Tour: Ethnographies of Travel*. Chicago: University of Chicago Press, 2005.

Calvino, I. *Le città invisibili* [*Invisible Cities*]. (W. Weaver, trans.). London: Vintage, 1997.

Council on International Educational Exchange (CIEE). "Down With America: Anti-Americanism and Study Abroad," 2009. Retrieved November 20, 2009, from http://www.ciee.org/study/advisors/anti-americanism.aspx

Cornwell, G. H., and Stoddard, E. W. *Globalizing Knowledge: Connecting International and Intercultural Studies*. Washington, D.C.: Association of American Colleges and Universities, 1999.

Cornwell, G. H., and Stoddard, E. W. "The Future of Liberal Education and the Hegemony of Market Values: Privilege, Practicality, and Citizenship." *Liberal Education*, 2001, *87(3)*, 6–15.

Davis, M. *City of Quartz*. London: Verso Press, 1998.

Dear, M. J. *The Postmodern Urban Condition*. Oxford: Blackwell, 2000.

Deardorff, D. K. "A Matter of Logic?" *International Educator*, 2005, *14(3)*, 26–31.

Deardorff, D. K. "Identification and Assessment of Intercultural Competence as a Student Outcome of Internationalization." *Journal of Studies in International Education*, 2006, *10(3)*, 241–266.

Deresiewicz, W. "Beyond Europe: The New Student Travel." *Chronicle of Higher Education*, July 20, 2009. Retrieved July 27, 2009, from http://chronicle.com/article/Beyond-Europe-the-New-Student/47105/

Edwards, J. "The 'Other Eden': Thoughts on American Study Abroad in Britain." *Frontiers: The International Journal of Study Abroad*, 2000, *4*(Winter), 83–98.

Foucault, M. "Des Espace Autres" ["Of Other Spaces"]. (J. Miskowiec, trans.). *Diacritics*, 1986, *16*, 22–27.

Glasson, J. "The Widening Local and Regional Development Impacts of the Modern Universities – A Tale of Two Cities (and North-South Perspectives)." *Local Economy*, 2003, *18(1)*, 21–37.

Gore, J. E. *Dominant Beliefs and Alternative Voices: Discourse, Belief, and Gender in American Study Abroad*. New York: Routledge, 2005.

Harvey, D. *The Condition of Postmodernity*. Oxford: Blackwell, 1990.

Hoffa, W. W. *A History of U.S. Study Abroad: Beginnings to 1965*. Carlisle, Pa.: The Forum on Education Abroad, Dickinson College, 2007.

Hovland, K. *Shared Futures: Global Learning and Liberal Education*. Washington, D.C.: Association of American Colleges and Universities, 2006.

Jellet, R., Toral, P., and Zipse, D. "Integrating Study Abroad into the Political Science Classroom." Paper presented at Integrating Study Abroad into the Undergraduate Curriculum: Transforming On-Campus Teaching and Learning, Beloit College, Beloit, Wis., November 2009.

Jones-Evans, D. "Entrepreneurial Universities: Policies, Strategies, and Practice." In P. Conceição, D. V. Gibson, H. V. Heitor, and S. Shariq (eds.), *Science, Technology, and Innovation Policy: Opportunities and Challenges for the Knowledge Economy.* Westport, Conn.: Quorum Books, 2000.

Lefebvre, H. *La production de l'espace* [*The Production of Space*]. (D. Nicholson-Smith, trans.). Oxford: Blackwell, 1994.

McBrien, J. L., and Brandt, R. S. *The Language of Learning: A Guide to Education Terms.* Alexandria, Va.: Association for Supervision and Curriculum Development, 1997.

Meacham, J., and Gaff, J. G. "Learning Goals in Mission Statements." *Liberal Education,* 2006, *92(1),* 6–13.

Mestenhauser, J. "Portraits of an International Curriculum: An Uncommon Multidimensional Perspective." In J. A. Mestenhauser and B. J. Ellingboe (eds.), *Reforming the Higher Education Curriculum: Internationalizing the Campus.* Phoenix, Ariz.: American Council on Education and Oryx Press, 1998.

Mestenhauser, J. A., and Ellingboe, B. J. (eds.). *Reforming the Higher Education Curriculum: Internationalizing the Campus.* Phoenix, Ariz.: American Council on Education and Oryx Press, 1998.

Osuagwu, N. G. *Facebook Addiction: The Life and Times of Social Networking Addicts.* New York: Ice Cream Melts Publishing, 2009.

Peterson, P. "The Worthy Goal of a Worldly Faculty." *Peer Review,* 2000, *3(1),* 3–7.

Selby, R. "Designing Transformation in International Education." In V. Savicki (ed.), *Developing Intercultural Competence and Transformation: Theory, Research, and Application in International Education.* Sterling, Va.: Stylus, 2008.

Sennett, R. *The Fall of Public Man.* London: Penguin, 1974.

Soja, E. W. *Postmodern Geographies, The Reassertion of Space in Critical Social Theory.* London & New York: Verso, 1989.

Stohl, M. "We Have Met the Enemy and He Is Us: The Role of Faculty in the Internationalization of Higher Education in the Coming Decade." *Journal of Studies in International Education,* 2007, *11(3/4),* 359–372.

Toral, P. "Synthesis and Career Preparation: The International Relations Senior Thesis." In B. Brewer and K. Cunningham (eds.), *Integrating Study Abroad into the Curriculum: Theory and Practice Across the Disciplines.* Sterling, Va.: Stylus, 2010.

Trooboff, S., Vande Berg, M., and Rayman, J. "Employer Attitudes Toward Study Abroad." *Frontiers: The Interdisciplinary Journal of Study Abroad,* 2007–2008, 15(Winter), 17–33.

Woolf, M. "Come and See the Poor People: The Pursuit of Exotica." *Frontiers: The Interdisciplinary Journal of Study Abroad,* 2006, 13, 135–146.

Zaslow, J. "The Greatest Generation (of Networkers)." *The Wall Street Journal,* Nov. 5, 2009. Retrieved November 5, 2009, from http://online.wsj.com/article/SB1000 14240527487047463045745056431535187087.html?mod=WSJ_hps_sections_lifestyle #printMode

Zukin, S. *Landscapes of Power: From Detroit to Disneyland.* Berkeley: University of California Press, 1991.

DARREN KELLY *is an instructor at St. Patrick's College, Dublin, Ireland, and faculty member at CEA Global Campus, Dublin.*

NEW DIRECTIONS FOR HIGHER EDUCATION • DOI: 10.1002/he

9

This chapter describes strategies that college leaders and faculty can use to develop international collaborations, questions that partners should consider prior to engaging in collaboration, and ways to avoid problems further into the process.

Strategies for Planning for the Future

L. Neal Holly

When I was working on my master's degree at a rural public university in North Carolina, I became enamored with the idea of working in a study-abroad office. I would travel around the world, negotiate articulation agreements with international counterparts, and help recruit students to my home institution. It would be ideal. I received an internship at the university's international office. I was disabused of my romantic notions and discovered that opportunities to travel abroad were rare and most of one's time instead dealt with mountains of paperwork that accompany incoming and outgoing students.

My experience occurred a decade ago when internationalization was more of an esoteric term. Today, the field of internationalization is a higher education juggernaut, at the tip of every president's tongue and a bullet point in every admissions brochure. International efforts permeate colleges and universities, impacting faculty work (Bottery, 2006), student learning (Bennett, 2008), and institutional operations (Eggins, 2003). International offices are one of the fastest growing components of colleges and universities. Yet, international efforts are often treated as disparate responsibilities rather than dealt with in a comprehensive and holistic approach (de Wit, 2002).

This chapter synthesizes the themes within the volume, focusing on the role of motivating factors and assumptions partners bring to international collaborations. Partners have different resources at their disposal and different levels of power to wield during negotiations and during the development process. Further, cross-border ventures create different issues based on the level of engagement. Leaders face particular challenges as they negotiate

NEW DIRECTIONS FOR HIGHER EDUCATION, no. 150, Summer 2010 © Wiley Periodicals, Inc.
Published online in Wiley InterScience (www.interscience.wiley.com) • DOI: 10.1002/he.394

partnerships, whereas faculty and students have their own sets of concerns emanating from their international forays. Finally, a series of questions and strategies are put forth as partners consider international collaborations.

Collaboration

Collaboration has emerged as the predominant theme in this volume. There have been many powerful examples of how faculty, administrators, and institutions have worked through trying times to develop agreements and polices that were mutually beneficial. Eddy (Chapter 2) explained how successful collaboration is essential whether it be at the national, system, institutional, or individual level. Creating new programs and developing international cooperation agreements can be daunting tasks. Supportive leaders are essential to hold together alliances, and motivate committees and staff members, especially, when a product can be years away. These individuals possess the institutional knowledge and social connections necessary to obtain financial and physical resources, and build approval for program goals throughout the community.

Collaborative efforts at the macro level, such as sweeping educational goals at the national level or handshake agreements between institutional leaders, may be the easy part to creating strong international partnerships. The devil may, indeed, live within the details, the micro-level components that must be achieved to reach a stage where students begin to matriculate in programs. What is included in the price of tuition? Where will students be housed? Where will they eat? If classes in English are not available, will students have access to tutors to help improve their language skills? Where will the student receive medical care and who is legally responsible for the costs? These are just a few of the issues that have to be worked out, and these co-curricular logistical items are far easier to resolve than those involving faculty and course content.

As Cooper and Mitsunaga (Chapter 6) point out, issues with partnerships can transcend logistical concerns and touch upon more unique issues, such as cultural differences between faculty members. Major philosophical differences can arise as well, especially in regards to how programs may ask faculty members to develop classes and assess students. For instance, successful completion of a course in Ireland would result in a student's receiving a 70 percent as opposed to an "A," and it may be difficult for American students to adjust to that grading approach. How this course work is incorporated into the student's transcript and into their curriculum is important. Therefore, it is crucial that these details are worked out in advance, to avoid students feeling penalized for studying abroad. It is not as simple as "we" or "they" must change, but both parties articulating their respective institutional academic philosophies and finding compromises. This agreement may be more difficult when working with individual faculty members, who feel that making academic concessions limit their ability to teach. As institutions become increasingly specific in educational outcomes for their students, they should consider the specific academic culture of the country and institutions involved, and work with their faculty to jointly develop outcomes. Improved communications technology, through teleconferencing and Internet-based video chat software, could be the key to resolving these finer points and create an atmosphere of ongoing dialogue between parties.

Technology continues to play a significant role in how institutions and individuals collaborate. What technological resources an educational system or institution has, particularly in the area of communication, could be the deciding factor if an institution wants to begin a relationship. Virtual tours of facilities and face-to-face telecommunications may eliminate the need for faculty or staff member to travel abroad as frequently. Instead of one person traveling to develop partnerships, teams of administrators, staff, students, alumni, and faculty from each institution could work together via the Internet as subcommittees or individuals to develop sections of an articulation agreement. The ability for each institution to offer this level of communication is an indicator of their resources, and offers each party valuable insight into how each team is organized and works together.

Behind the scenes of international efforts is the administrative infrastructure, with the first line of impact occurring at the department level. As Amey (Chapter 5) illustrated, many international partnerships begin due to faculty work in international contexts. This type of work does not occur in a vacuum, however, especially as departmental and college resources are committed to allow the partnership to flourish. Internal policy decisions must be made, in particular regarding the commitment of resources. Initial partnership development may occur on the individual level, but sustainable partnerships require institutionalization of policies and procedures (Amey, Eddy, and Campbell, 2010). An assessment of divisional and departmental resources and goals that proceeds the development of articulation policies and procedures could help avoid internal administrative struggles. This evaluation may indicate the institution lacks the necessary funding to launch or support a new venture or that other ongoing institutional or individual efforts are more of a priority and require dedicated resources instead. Consequently, adding on a new international partnership may not be feasible for faculty and staff in the short term. It is important to engage in dialogue about the vision of the project to determine what is required for support and sustainability of proposed collaborations.

Timing (and Resources) Is Everything

As we have read in this volume, dynamic growth of international efforts has led to growing pains, whether in regards to alliances, third parties, institutional offices, or forces beyond the institution. An institution could have an excellent partner, great leadership, an ideal plan, and all of it falls apart. For example, Loyalist College was more than ready to accept students from China, but immigration regulations became a major obstacle in attracting Chinese students to Canada. In the Loyalist case, it took years and the help of a third party to create a successful partnership model. And as Holland noted (Chapter 3), the partnership is a work in progress with time dedicated to maintaining relationships and assuring quality of student learning.

Loyalist College became increasingly interested in internationalization as a pathway to increase revenues. In the United States, most international students do not qualify for any federal assistance. In fact, unless there is institutional aid available, and even exchange rates (which are quickly disappearing), or some subsidy from their home country, many international students pay the full price of attendance. In the age of cash-starved institutions and systems, international students constitute a financial windfall. In Australia, foreign students have become the nation's third largest export, with over 350,000 students attending in 2006 (Baker, 2006). Marginson (2006) contends that the current absence of higher education in developing countries is an opportunity that nations, like Australia, should take advantage of before those same developing nations "catch-up," especially in areas such as health sciences and technology.

How an institution delves into international programming may very well depend on its resources, both human and financial. As Jie found (Chapter 4), the motivations to partner may shift over time resulting in different views of the benefits of collaboration. Developing handshake agreements with an institution abroad is one matter, having staff to help coordinate orientations, paperwork, and recruitment is another. Depending on the type of program and financial resources, it may be easier to let a third party handle the agreements and logistics. A smaller institution with not as many students traveling abroad may opt to give students fewer options and promote group-level programs. A larger institution with more resources may develop a program mission to encourage individuals to pursue studies wherever possible. To facilitate such a widespread approach to student travel, international offices place much of the administrative burden on the students, asking them to book travel, assure that their courses will transfer back to their home institution, and make sure that all of their documents are in order. Not only does such an approach relieve logistical pressure on support staff, but this also helps the student develop the frame of mind necessary to be successful abroad.

Resources extend beyond travel options and logistics. Programmatic resources play a vital role in supporting the curricular outcomes of any experience. A more-focused preparation period allows students to begin acclimatizing to the academic culture of the destination institution. The Cities in Transition program outlined by Brewer (Chapter 7) provides just this opportunity for Beloit students before they travel abroad. Students may not be aware of foreign faculty members' disposition towards instructor/student relationships or the use of technology in the classroom. Understanding these nuances before an experience begins can reduce conflict and

NEW DIRECTIONS FOR HIGHER EDUCATION • DOI: 10.1002/he

confusion for the student and the faculty member. Not only do students gain a better understanding of the academic culture of another institution and country, but faculty members who see a reduction in culture clashes may be more open to new suggestions on outcomes and techniques. Conversely, the same students will need assistance in transitioning back to their home institution. Now the student has become an academic resource. Faculty should utilize these students' experiences and those of their international counterparts, in the classroom, especially at smaller institutions where faculty are more aware of which students have study-abroad opportunities.

Unique is Good

In an era in which many higher education institutions and their components are becoming so similar, international programs are refreshingly unique. Each institution's curricular and co-curricular standards, their distinctive relationships with others, and the pathways in which those relationships were developed, make that shared program like no other. Having no direct model to base a new program on can be a challenge, but this has led individuals and teams to explore the landscape of options that institutions have in order that they may find the best fit for themselves. As the field continues to develop best practices, how can it avoid a "one size fits all" approach? Perhaps the complexity of these relationships will make it impossible to replicate a particular partnership with others. As leaders and institutions learn from each experience, they are able to take and utilize pieces of what they have learned into their next partnership. They can also collaborate with others through networks and professional organizations to share this information so that others can avoid pitfalls, not to directly replicate their efforts.

Internationalization efforts also offer a unique opportunity to unite the curricular and co-curricular divisions on campus. International offices are located in a strategic "crossroads" between academic affairs and campus divisions. As internationalization efforts have grown on-campus, offices have developed strong relationships and have developed the power to bring a diverse mix of campus interests to one table. Often faculty, who are troubled by instructional changes, may not be aware that professionals in the student counseling department or housing office are also dealing with similar changes to how they provide services. Both domestic and international students can feel frustrated by mismatches in curricular policies. When developing partnerships, academic outcomes for students' abroad experiences should also be aligned with co-curricular and shared outcomes. Not only would this combination outcome be beneficial in helping partner institutions' faculty understand the context and need for such objectives, but it would also help the home institution develop a more holistic internationalization framework for students who are traveling abroad and for those matriculating to the United States. Such a framework could, for example, focus on how the international experience could be utilized by faculty and staff programmatically before, during, and after a student has studied abroad. Every institution has different focus areas, missions, and resources. Therefore, each institution should evaluate how to best take advantage of internationalization as a holistic opportunity.

Institutional partnerships are unique entities onto themselves. Key to international partnerships are outlining goals and objectives of the venture. As noted in this book, partner resources, goals, and vision may differ among collaborators. Therefore, identifying roles and expectations will avoid misunderstandings that may derail the collaboration. Leaders play a role at the inception stage as they show support for the partnership, whereas faculty champions bring high levels of social capital to these ventures that bring others together. Faculty members also serve as the bridge between student learners and administration. In this capacity, they create curriculums, identify student learning goals, and deliver course content to students. Every level involved in a partnership brings a unique contribution, but it is important to note that all are critical for ultimate success.

Future Considerations

It is an exciting time to be a part of and study the evolving field of international education. As new ventures are created, it is important to address several important considerations. Many questions remain unanswered: What are students learning and how do institutions incorporate that experience into the "home" curriculum? How do we measure what is considered a life-altering experience by many students? Who are the students involved in study abroad and is it an inclusive sample of an institution's enrollment? How do institutions with fewer resources compete for partnerships and facilities abroad with those with unimaginable coffers? How will advancing communication technologies change study-abroad programs? Finally, how does internationalization challenge the traditional institutional frameworks and roles?

Those seeking international partnerships can benefit from considering the questions outlined above. Underpinning these ventures is the notion that students need to become more globally competent given our global economy and linked economic systems. More students are traveling abroad now than ever, but faculty still lag behind their international counterparts in engagement in international work (Finkelstein, Walker, and Chen, 2009). Efforts in faculty development, such as those outlined by Brewer in Chapter 7, are central to increasing faculty engagement, and ultimately impacting student learning. Likewise, it is important to consider the student learning experience. Kelly (Chapter 8) points out that students understand their time abroad in an ambi-location and institutions need to be intentional about engaging students fully in the foreign country's culture. In the following section, several resources are outlined for those considering international partnerships. Planning ahead can help avoid missteps others have experienced and set the foundation for a successful collaboration.

Additional Resources

Web Sites

Association of International Educators (NAFSA)
  http://www.nafsa.org/
The Council for International Educational Exchange
  http://www.ciee.org/
The Council for International Exchange of Scholars
  http://www.cies.org/
International Student Exchange Programs
  http://www.isep.org/
The U.S. Department of State: Bureau of Educational and Cultural Affairs
  http://exchanges.state.gov/

Publications on Developing Programs and Partnerships

Althen, G. *Learning Across Cultures.* Annapolis Junction, Md.: NAFSA, 1994.
Brewer, E., and Cunningham, K. (eds.). *Integrating Study Abroad into the Curriculum: Theory and Practice Across the Disciplines.* Sterling, Va.: Stylus, 2010.
Brockington, J. L., Hoffa, W. W., and Martin, P. C. (eds.). *Guide to Education Abroad* (3rd ed.). Annapolis Junction, Md.: NAFSA, 2005.
de Wit, H. (ed.). *The Journal of Studies in International Education.* Newbury Park, Calif.: Sage Publications.
Lamet, M. *Abroad by Design.* Annapolis Junction, Md.: NAFSA, 2000.
NAFSA. *Internationalizing the Campus* (2003 – Present). The report each year highlights the winner of the Senator Paul Simon Award for Campus Internationalization. The 2008 report can be viewed online via http://www.nafsa.org/_/File/_/itc2008.pdf

References

Amey, M. J. "Administrative Perspectives on International Partnerships." New Directions for Higher Education, no. 150. San Francisco: Jossey-Bass, 2010.
Amey, M. J., Eddy, P. L., and Campbell, T. G. "Crossing Boundaries: Creating Community College Partnerships to Promote Educational Transitions." *Community College Review,* 2010, 37(4), 333–347.
Baker, J. "University Brand Power." *Australasian Business Intelligence,* 2006, 28(45), 19.
Bennett, J. "On Becoming a Global Soul: A Path to Engagement During Study Abroad." In V. Savicki (ed.), *Developing Intercultural Competence and Transformation: Theory, Research, and Application in International Education.* Sterling, Va.: Stylus, 2008.
Bottery, M. "Education and Globalization: Redefining the Role of the Educational Professional." *Educational Review,* 2006, 58(1), 95–113.
Brewer, E. "Leveraging Partnerships to Internationalize the Liberal Arts College: Campus Internationalization and the Faculty." New Directions for Higher Education, no. 150. San Francisco: Jossey-Bass, 2010.
Cooper, J., and Mitsunaga, R. "Faculty Perspectives on International Education: The Nested Realities of Faculty Collaborations." New Directions for Higher Education, no. 150. San Francisco: Jossey-Bass, 2010.
de Wit, H. *Internationalization of Higher Education in the United States of America and Europe: A Historical, Comparative, and Conceptual Analysis.* Westport, Conn.: Greenwood Press, 2002.
Eddy, P. L. "Institutional Collaborations in Ireland: Leveraging an Increased International Presence." New Directions for Higher Education, no. 150. San Francisco: Jossey-Bass, 2010.

Eggins, H. "Globalization and Reform: Necessary Conjunctions in Higher Education." In H. Eggins (ed.), *Globalization and Reform in Higher Education*. Berkshire, UK: Open University Press, 2003.

Finkelstein, M. J., Walker, E., and Chen, R. "The Internationalization of the American Faculty: Where Are We? What Drives or Deters Us?" Unpublished report, Seton Hall University, South Orange, N.J., 2009.

Holland, D. "Notes from the Field: Lessons Learned in Building a Framework for an International Collaboration." New Directions for Higher Education, no. 150. San Francisco: Jossey-Bass, 2010.

Jie, Y. "International Partnerships: A Game Theory Perspective." New Directions for Higher Education, no. 150. San Francisco: Jossey-Bass, 2010.

Kelly, D. "Student Learning in an International Setting." New Directions for Higher Education, no. 150. San Francisco: Jossey-Bass, 2010.

Marginson, S. "Dynamics of National and Global Competition." *Higher Education*, 2006, *52(1)*, 1–39.

L. NEAL HOLLY *is a research assistant and doctoral student in the Educational Policy, Planning, and Leadership-Higher Education Administration program in the School of Education at the College of William and Mary.*

INDEX

ORDER FORM SUBSCRIPTION AND SINGLE ISSUES

DISCOUNTED BACK ISSUES:

Use this form to receive 20% off all back issues of *New Directions for Higher Education*.
All single issues priced at **$23.20** (normally $29.00)

TITLE	ISSUE NO.	ISBN
_____	_____	_____
_____	_____	_____
_____	_____	_____

Call 888-378-2537 or see mailing instructions below. When calling, mention the promotional code JBXND to receive your discount. For a complete list of issues, please visit www.josseybass.com/go/ndhe

SUBSCRIPTIONS: (1 YEAR, 4 ISSUES)

☐ New Order   ☐ Renewal

U.S.	☐ Individual: $89	☐ Institutional: $244
CANADA/MEXICO	☐ Individual: $89	☐ Institutional: $284
ALL OTHERS	☐ Individual: $113	☐ Institutional: $318

Call 888-378-2537 or see mailing and pricing instructions below.
Online subscriptions are available at www.interscience.wiley.com

ORDER TOTALS:

Issue / Subscription Amount: $ _____

Shipping Amount: $ _____
(for single issues only – subscription prices include shipping)

Total Amount: $ _____

SHIPPING CHARGES:		
SURFACE	DOMESTIC	CANADIAN
First Item	$5.00	$6.00
Each Add'l Item	$3.00	$1.50

(No sales tax for U.S. subscriptions. Canadian residents, add GST for subscription orders. Individual rate subscriptions must be paid by personal check or credit card. Individual rate subscriptions may not be resold as library copies.)

BILLING & SHIPPING INFORMATION:

☐ **PAYMENT ENCLOSED:** *(U.S. check or money order only. All payments must be in U.S. dollars.)*

☐ **CREDIT CARD:**   ☐ VISA   ☐ MC   ☐ AMEX

Card number _____Exp. Date_____

Card Holder Name_____Card Issue # *(required)* _____

Signature _____Day Phone_____

☐ **BILL ME:** *(U.S. institutional orders only. Purchase order required.)*

Purchase order # _____
Federal Tax ID 13559302 • GST 89102-8052

Name_____

Address_____

Phone_____ E-mail_____

Copy or detach page and send to: **John Wiley & Sons, PTSC, 5th Floor**
989 Market Street, San Francisco, CA 94103-1741

Order Form can also be faxed to: **888-481-2665**

PROMO JBXND